Before I Thee Wed

A guide to help engaged couples
prepare for marriage.

Before I Thee Wed

A guide to help engaged couples
prepare for marriage.

CAROLYN SHEALY SELF
and
WILLIAM L. SELF

Power Books

Fleming H. Revell Company
Old Tappan, New Jersey

TO all engaged couples—Nearlyweds
May God richly bless you and prepare you for the
exciting life you will build together as marriage
partners.

Scripture identified NIV is from the Holy Bible, New International
Version. Copyright © 1973, 1978, 1984 International Bible Society.
Used by permission of Zondervan Bible Publishers.

Scripture identified RSV is from the Revised Standard Version of the
Bible, Copyrighted © 1946, 1952, 1971, by the Division of Christian
Education of the National Council of the Churches of Christ in the
United States of America, and is used by permission. All rights
reserved.

Library of Congress Cataloging-in-Publication Data

Self, Carolyn Shealy.
   Before I thee wed : a guide to help engaged couples prepare for
marriage / Carolyn Shealy Self and William L. Self.
      p.   cm.
   ISBN 0-8007-5315-1
   1. Family life education—United States. 2. Marriage—United States.
3. Marriage—Religious aspects—Christianity. 4. Marriage counseling—United States. I. Self, William L.   II. Title.
HQ10.5.U6S45   1989
646.7′ 8--dc20   89-8447
                                                                    CIP

Copyright © 1989 by Carolyn Shealy Self and William L. Self
Published by the Fleming H. Revell Company
Old Tappan, New Jersey 07675
Printed in the United States of America

Table of Contents

Acknowledgments

Jack Naish, Minister of Education at Wieuca Road Baptist Church, gave us the idea of this special ministry to Newlywed/ Newly Rewed couples almost ten years ago. He has expanded the vision of ministry to specialty groups throughout the church, and we appreciate and applaud his vision and support.

Dick and Betty Henshaw, teachers of our Nearlywed class, have gone beyond the call of duty in their preparation of lessons that laid a foundation for this book. Wayne and Jenny Pee have been their faithful helpers and good examples for their peers. Without their help and the support of the other "Nearlywed/Newlywed" staff, we could never have had such a successful and exciting experience. Many thanks to each of you.

Without the help of Miriam Childs, our manuscript would never have been typed into readable form. We appreciate all the hours she spent deciphering our scrawled words.

Norma and Bill Key, our patient readers, unscrambled some of our thoughts and straightened out some very crooked sentences! They have a vested interest in our ministry to engaged couples as the leaders of our Newlywed group.

To the Nearlyweds, the engaged couples who have been our test group, we are deeply indebted to you for your participation and helpful suggestions. Thank you for your willingness to launch a new ministry.

We would also like to say thank you to our friends and family who have been patient with our busy schedule. Thank you all for your understanding and support.

Introduction

The seeds of this book were planted a number of years ago by a friend whose daughter had had a disastrous marriage. She said, "You do so much for young couples *after* they are married (referring to our Church School Seminar for newlyweds), why don't you have a seminar for engaged couples? Maybe my Mary would not have made such a terrible mistake."

Maybe so, maybe not. Mary, like other young women and men who are starry-eyed and blissful, often refuse to heed even obvious danger signs observed by those who love them dearly. The disturbing fact is that approximately fifty percent of the couples who are now marrying will get divorced. I believe that if an engaged couple will commit themselves to four to six months exploring the topics in this book, they will either decide not to get married, or, if they do, they will be much better prepared for marriage's inevitable difficulties.

In October of 1987, we announced a special Church School class for "Nearlyweds." It was an instant success in the sense that engaged couples seemed to appear out of nowhere. We have been blessed to have as the leaders of this class a couple who helped us start our first "Newlywed" class over ten years ago. Dick and Betty Henshaw are wonderful role models. They have the rare gift of commitment and the ability to be very flexible—to "hang loose." The Henshaws have three adult children; right now their son and his fiancée are participating in this group. They have also had the help of a fine young couple, Wayne and Jenny Pee, to keep up with couples, make contacts, and represent the young married situations.

One of the difficulties in maintaining this class is the fact that couples join when they become engaged; sometimes they are not there very long if the engagement is a short one. However, the Henshaws do an amazing job of providing each couple with

8

an overview of the most important topics. After they are married, the couples go to our Newlywed Seminar, which picks up where our class leaves off.

During the course of a year, we determined the subjects that seemed most important and "brainstormed" the curriculum. The chapters in this book are the result of our study. We explore the issues that most newlyweds will face. We have had several couples postpone their weddings as a result of this seminar. We do not consider that failure. We are happy, rather, that they broke up an engagement instead of a marriage.

My husband and the other staff ministers do as much premarital counseling as they can. However, it is more helpful for a couple to be surrounded by peers who are experiencing the same things, and to participate in discussions over a longer period of time. This gives the extra help that many couples need. It also provides a way to make new friends as a couple.

Bill and I have two hopes for this book; they are stated in the part titles. First, we hope that engaged couples will examine their emotions, and second, having done so, that they will be prepared to meet the inevitable problems and joys of married life secure in the knowledge that their marriage is forever.

Suggested Ways to Use This Book for Seminars, Group Counseling, and Individual Couples

MARRIAGE AND FAMILY LIFE COUNSELORS may use this material for individual or group counseling for engaged couples. Each couple should have a copy of the book to use between sessions. The composition of your counseling group (which could range from very young couples approaching their first marriage, to older "first time" couples, to couples in which one or both partners have been previously married) will determine the chapters most needed by the entire group. Separate counseling sessions may be scheduled for those who need additional chapters.

We have found that one of the most effective ways to conduct a group counseling situation is to divide the participants into small groups (no more than five) to discuss a pertinent question. Their suggestions for problem resolutions will guide your presentation. This promotes dialogue and gives them the opportunity to express ideas and feelings in a protected environment. Depending on the topic, we may separate the couples so that each partner will feel free to express him or herself.

These sessions can also be used to help each couple to develop their communication skills. Some of the FOR YOU TO DO sections may be done in the presence of the group or under your guidance.

Couples who are open to premarital counseling and who will participate in a group situation will be much better equipped for marriage. There is a possibility that some will decide to break their engagement or postpone the wedding. The leader may feel badly about this but, realistically, it is a blessing. You have provided guidance and a setting where the couple can openly and realistically look at their situation. Of course, if they decide to break up or postpone marriage, you will be needed to help each one through the grief process. You will find some suggestions for group activities in many of the chapters.

CHURCH SCHOOL TEACHERS AND LEADERS will find this material useful for an ongoing class with young adults. As the single adults in your church become engaged, this class would help them bridge the gap between single and married. When used regularly as a Church School class, this course becomes a wonderful outreach tool.

Leaders for this group must be very flexible as well as warm and caring. In our Church School class for engaged couples, we allow couples to enter the class as soon as they are engaged and remain until the wedding date. (After the wedding, we also have a Newlywed class for them.) It won't matter what chapter you are on when they enter. You will know your group well enough to identify specific needs and choose appropriate chapters as your group comes and goes. As I said, flexibility will be the key in making this group a success.

We think that it is better for a couple who have been married for some time (at least ten to fifteen years) to teach this class. Young couples need good role models and this class is an unusual opportunity to provide them. The couple who helped us create this class have children ranging in age from twenty-six to thirty-three years old and are very aware of life-style, interests, and needs of this age group. We also have a young couple (married about four years) who help by keeping in touch with everyone, keeping records of who is in the class, wedding dates, etc., participating in class discussion, and relating as peers to the group. Both of these couples are blessed with a wonderful sense of humor and use it to advantage.

You will find Scripture references for many of the chapters in the helps at the end of the book. The chapter on religion will provide an opportunity to encourage couples to start out with a church relationship and to feel comfortable praying with each other. This will strengthen their relationship and deepen their intimacy.

INDIVIDUAL COUPLES will enjoy using this book as a

springboard for discussions about topics that they are concerned about but may hesitate to bring up. If they can agree to go through the book, talk about each chapter, and complete the FOR YOU TO DO sections, many gray areas can be cleared up. Don't hesitate to make notes or write answers in your book. It will be interesting to go back in later years to look at problem areas and see how changes may have come. The time set aside for this realistic look at yourselves may be the most important thing you do as an engaged couple.

We suggest that couples set a designated time at least once a week to talk about the chapters that you have read. Be sure that you will not be rushed or interrupted. It is important for each of you to listen carefully to the other. If one seems uneasy about a certain topic, go back to it later. It may signal future problems.

Allow yourself plenty of time to finish the book before the rush of wedding parties begins. Begin also to search for a social group of engaged and newly married couples that you both enjoy. Mutual friends will be an important influence in your life. We hope that you will find a compatible group in your church. If you will be using this book without the guidance of a counselor or group leader, let me explain the purpose of the FOR YOU TO DO sections at the end of each chapter. The value of the material will be enhanced if you set aside an hour or two each week to "test" yourselves by participating in the exercises. You are affirming your commitment to your financé(e) when you give your undivided attention to the development of this important relationship. After all, it is intended to last a lifetime but it won't happen magically.

Be sure to find a comfortable place, preferably where you can look at each other. Have pencils and paper at hand, answer the questions honestly and individually, then compare notes and discuss your answers.

We suggest this because all the subjects in this book are important for engaged couples to discuss, but many people are afraid to bring them up on their own. Using the book helps couples to confront difficult topics without being embarrassed.

One more suggestion: Try to be honest, reflecting your own views, not those of your parents or friends. This is strictly private business . . . the beginning of your exclusive relationship.

PART I

Emotions Tested (Where Are You Now?)

1

What Is Marriage?

Many of our favorite old fairy tales have this ending: "So they were married and lived happily ever after." And this is what many of us would like to think about marriage . . . happily ever after. However, we all know from divorce statistics and the brokenhearted letters to advice columns that many couples do not achieve marital happiness.

There may be more divorces today, but that doesn't necessarily mean that there is more unhappiness in marriage. We have no idea how many couples one or two generations ago stayed together because it was impossible for them to separate. People who are ready to get married have been dreaming some private dreams of love and happiness. The movies and love stories would have us believe that happy marriage is something handed as a gift to us on our wedding day. Actually, a happy marriage is something to be created together through many years of loving, caring, nurturing, and "hanging in there" through good times and bad.

Marriage is a beautiful, life-consuming relationship. Other than your relationship to God, marriage is the most important relationship you will ever have. It is worth all of the time, energy, sacrifice, and devotion you can put into it.

If you are not a happy person now, if you feel that life has cheated you and you are counting on marriage to be a state of bliss that requires no effort on your part, you will be very disappointed. Your unhappiness will multiply. You will continue to be miserable and will spread your unhappiness to your spouse and any children you may have. You have a much greater chance for marital happiness if you have learned to be responsible for your own happiness. You cannot depend on anyone else to make you happy.

Marriage Commitment

Marriage is a commitment. It is the commitment of your life to someone else. Marriage is an unconditional commitment and not a contract. In most contracts, there are certain conditions. For example, the contract may state that "if you do this, the other person must do that." In the marriage commitment, there is no escape clause.

A commitment is a binding pledge or promise, a private pledge that you also make public. Commitment involves the total giving of yourself to another person. This involves a great deal of risk, but life is very dull when you take no risks. Only with this risk can you know the joy of deep, abiding love and fulfillment.

This commitment, to be true and faithful to each other for the rest of your lives, will require daily attention and nurture. It must never be taken for granted or pushed to the background to make room for other commitments. Your parents, children, profession—everything except your commitment to God—must come after your marital commitment to each other. It must be your primary relationship.

Good Marriage Prospect

Who is a good marriage prospect? Dr. David Mace, well-known marriage counselor, describes this person as one who is cooperative in his attitude toward other people. He (she) works well with those in authority over him, is kind and sympathetic toward his inferiors, and ready to help anyone in trouble. He (she) is conventional in his attitude about abiding by rules and obeying the law. He is friendly with members of the opposite sex and treats them as equals. He is at ease in a gathering of people. In contrast, the person likely to be an unhappy marriage partner is described this way: He (she) is ill at ease in social settings and feels inferior. He (she) tends to be "bossy" and domineering when in a superior position. He hates to be in competition because he is a bad loser. He doesn't like taking orders from others and tends to be negative and a chronic complainer.

Few people conform perfectly to these descriptions of successful or unsuccessful marriage prospects. However, they are a helpful guide to determine if you are able to successfully negotiate the joys and the difficulties of an intimate relationship.

Love and Marriage

The most happily married couples are those who love each other deeply. You will never hear a really loving couple talk about separation or divorce. Married love is much like the love of friendship. It is the desire to be together whatever life may bring. It includes the desire to cherish and care for each other and also a certain amount of sacrificial love. Sexual love is important because it is the supreme expression of married love, which, when properly used, strengthens the marriage bond.

The marriage relationship is different from all other relationships in that men and women are made for each other. God planned it this way. There is a kind of magnetic attraction that draws a man and a woman together. The Bible says that in marriage the two become one flesh. This is a beautiful picture of how close and how treasured this marriage relationship should be.

All kinds of people get married. Even when a marriage ends in a divorce, the participants are usually ready to try again. This is a tribute to the institution and to our expectation of happiness within a good marriage. It is noted that of all Americans who are old enough to get married, ninety-six percent will be married at some point in their lives. The pity is that such a small percentage will put out the effort to make theirs a truly superior relationship.

Sam and Joan were having a great time in our Newlywed Seminar. They were enjoying participating in the discussions, and their enthusiasm infected the whole group. One day as we were walking to the parking lot together, Joan turned to me with shining eyes and exclaimed, "I just love being married to Sam. We have the most fun and I'm always discovering something new about him." The enthusiasm that Sam and Joan have for their life together will allow them to continually discover new depths in each other, enhancing their ability to truly understand and be understood by the most important person in their lives.

Marriage is what we make of it from day to day. It is a work of art and you are the artists. This is your opportunity to use every bit of your creativity to make this canvas a thing of great beauty for all to admire and enjoy.

For You to Do

1. You won't need paper or pencil for this question. Think about the marriages in your family: your parents, grandparents, aunts and uncles, etc. Are there any that you admire? Tell each other about them.
2. If any of your friends are married, think about what you observe in their marriages. Are some of them good? Tell each other about them.
3. Think about the marriage you want. Tell each other what your heart's desire for marriage is. Listen carefully.
4. Complete this sentence for each other: I love you because. . . .

2

What Is Engagement?

Being betrothed, or engaged to be married, is a custom as old as the Bible. We find the term used concerning Joseph and Mary (Matthew 1:18), as well as in the Old Testament concerning the relationship of God to Israel (Hosea 2:29).

Webster's Dictionary defines engagement as a pledge, an obligation, or agreement, a giving of one's word or promise to be true. This is an important step and should never be taken lightly. The engagement time should be used to test your ability to be faithful to your fiancé(e).

The Engagement Period

Christmas seems to be a favorite time to announce an engagement. Perhaps that is why June is traditionally such a popular month for weddings. Actually, the three summer months and December are almost equally popular for weddings. There is no "proper" time for the length of an engagement, but certainly a specific date should be set as soon as possible so that plans can be made without being rushed.

Six to eight months is the usual length of a formal engagement. Of course, the couple has probably been dating each other exclusively for some time before the formal engagement is announced. Our son and daughter-in-law became engaged and were married in a large church wedding within two months. What a lot had to be accomplished! They had been dating for several years, so their relationship was not new and their work and school schedules suddenly cleared for them to marry. Whether your engagement is long or short will depend on many things, but it is very important to use the time to benefit your coming marriage. More important than any of the details of the ceremony is the planning for the success of your marriage relationship.

The engagement period should be long enough for you to get used to the idea of being married. Marriage is a complex and demanding relationship which requires constant tending. It is not the cure-all for life's problems, but will be what you make of it. Many responsibilities come with marriage and many times one or both partners feel overwhelmed. Generally speaking, this is normal. However, if the feeling continues over a period of time, you should seek counseling to talk it through. Most people go through a brief time of doubt, but love for the person will overcome these feelings.

A Testing Time

This book should give you some specific ways to use your engagement to explore the issues that will vitally affect your marriage. It is our hope that by testing your emotions and examining your motives and ideas now, your relationship will continually surpass your highest expectations.

Engagement is a time for you to test your maturity. Couples seem to be older chronologically when they get married than people used to be. In the fifties, girls graduating from college without definite plans to marry were rare. They were afraid that love had passed them by! Today, people are more concerned with getting their careers going and becoming independent individuals "on their own." Only time will tell if these later marriages survive better than those begun by couples in their early twenties.

We all know that age really doesn't have much to do with a person's maturity. A lot of people have great struggles with leaving the parental nest even though they may be very successful in their careers. Sometimes a person who is success- ful in business develops a very self-centered and selfish life-style. He/she will have a difficult time adjusting to the give and take of the marriage relationship.

Maturity covers a lot of territory, as you will see in this book. As you study it, you will be able to view marriage in a more realistic way. The better prepared you are for problems that may occur, the better able you will be to adjust and not panic when conflicts arise.

Wanted: Maturity

I remember so well the day that Ben, a special family friend, called to say that he had to talk to us. Ben had been married for ten years to his childhood sweetheart and they had two children, a boy and a girl. Now they had been divorced for a number of years. Immaturity is probably never used as a reason for divorce, but I'm sure that all their differences stemmed from that one problem: their mutual immaturity.

Ben sat at our dinner table bubbling over with the news that he had just met, five days earlier, the woman he was going to marry! She was gorgeous, had a great career, three young children by a previous marriage, and best of all, thought that he was her dream man! Well, we could hardly wait to meet this wonderful person, and in a couple of days we arranged to have both Ben and Jane over for dinner. He was right. She was all of the things he had claimed and she adored him! They married within six short weeks. We were worried and afraid for them but they refused to listen to any of their friends. Arranging the wedding should have warned them that they had totally different ideas about things and that they did not resolve problems easily, but they did not see the warning signs.

I wish I had a happy ending to this story. In less than six months, Jane decided that for her health and the well-being of her children, she would seek a divorce. It was an unusually stormy and almost violent relationship, yet they still felt a strong physical attachment. Ben went on to remarry his first wife and divorced her again. Jane has had a series of short-lived romances. They are both now well into their forties but are no more mature in their relationships than they were fifteen years ago.

Communication Patterns

Use your engagement to assess your own maturity level and that of your intended spouse. This period should be long enough to allow you to learn some basic communication skills. You'll need them to calmly and intelligently discuss matters such as money management, social obligations, friends, sex, and household chores. These things need to be addressed before marriage, though adjustments can be made along the way. Learn to talk honestly and openly without being confrontational. Set positive patterns for dealing with problems and learn to recognize potentially difficult areas. Try to develop communication patterns that can accommodate both of you in a positive way. By all means, remain flexible and don't lose your sense of humor! If you can laugh WITH each other, not AT each other, you can overcome large hurdles.

Wedding Plans

Once you have set the date for the wedding, the stress begins! An important thing for the bride-to-be to remember is that this wedding is really a statement that your parents will make to their friends. Whether you like it or not, parents see their children as an extension of themselves. They want things perfect for their children. They will be more nervous over this whole thing than you will. Try to be patient. When he does pre-marital counseling, my husband always tells the bride that she should remember that this is really her parents' wedding; she should just relax and let them enjoy it!

Siblings often try to be the center of attention at such a time. All the old rivalry and jealousy of childhood comes out to parade down the aisle along with the wedding party.

Planning the wedding and executing it calls for the utmost courtesy on the part of every person. It is everyone's responsibility to make this a happy time, one that will be remembered with pleasure.

Some practical matters that need prompt attention include:

- Get the date settled and the church reserved as soon as possible. Most churches have rules concerning the use of the facilities. Abide by them cheerfully.
- Respect the minister's schedule concerning pre-marital counseling and rehearsal time. Many ministers do not rehearse weddings. The wedding director or wedding committee of the church will perform that function.
- If your church does not have a wedding director, most large department stores offer that service.
- Purchase a good handbook on how to plan the type of wedding you desire. Establish a schedule to get things done.
- The bridal registry of your local department store and your bridal salon will have consultants to answer your questions and help you get organized.
- Get organized!

Remember that every bride is beautiful and every wedding is special in its own way. Relax and enjoy!

For You to Do

Each of you should answer these questions and then compare notes.

1. Are you a happy, well-adjusted person?
2. Can you handle difficult or trying situations? Illustrate with one or two instances.
3. How long have you known each other? How well do you know each other? Tell each other something that you think he/she doesn't know about you.
4. Do you like each other? This is different than love. Tell each other something special that you like about him/her.
5. Are you mature enough to get married? Is your fiancé(e) mature enough to get married?
6. Are you willing to take the time and energy to study this book and openly discuss the topics with your intended spouse?
7. What kind of wedding do you want? What can you afford? Will your parents be able to help finance all or most of the wedding?
8. Who do you want to perform the ceremony? Do you and your intended agree? How many attendants will you have? Who will they be?
9. Are you ready to talk to your parents about your plans?

3

What Is Love?

There is a familiar song that says, "I love you for sentimental reasons." It is a beautiful, romantic song designed for easy listening as well as pleasant communication. However, when we get past the romance of a relationship, we need to explore this word "love" that is used so often.

One definition of love describes it as "the respect, recognition, consideration, and care of other persons." A mutually loving relationship is a constantly growing, changing, challenging experience for both parties. The only way a mature love can be nurtured is for each partner to know himself and to be aware of his own needs, feelings, and experiences. Jesus said to love your neighbor as yourself. You need to know who you are under the mask in order to be able to love another person.

Love exists when the satisfaction or security of another person becomes as significant to you as your own. Love means to commit yourself without a guarantee that your love will be returned. Love is an act of faith, not demanding anything in return.

Three Kinds of Love

There are three forms of love in our lives. The first is eros, or need love (erotic love). This is romantic, sexual love, inspired by the biology of our human nature. Eros is sometimes equated with infatuation, but this is not love that will last. Eros is a passionate desire for your loved one; this love is certainly needed for a satisfying and fulfilling marriage.

However, for love to endure, it has to move beyond eros to the second level of love, phileo, or friendship. This is usually known as brotherly love. However, it is basically a relationship that involves closely working together on a project. In this case, the project would be the relationship of marriage; the couple is working as one in this common interest.

The third type of love that a marriage needs is agape love. This is a self-giving love—love that goes on loving even when the other person is unlovable. Love is a personal act of commitment; it is not something that just happens to you. Agape love can rekindle the flame of eros, or erotic love, or keep it alive in a relationship that is based on committed love. This love allows us to overcome irritability and selfishness as we desire to meet the needs of our mate. It should be a healthy desire to be mutually fulfilling, for each to seek the best interest of the other.

Romantic love, as it matures, becomes caring love that can last a lifetime, through all the trials, sicknesses, frustrations, and problems that life normally brings.

Long-Term Love

The most beautiful and poignant love stories are those of lovers who have faced life and endured. Until about two years ago, I could look out my kitchen window every afternoon and see my neighbors, in their early nineties, strolling hand in hand up and down the street, getting their exercise. They went hand in hand through life for over sixty-five years and were still sweet to each other. The husband bragged about his wife's accomplishments every chance he got. His wife would respond warmly that he was her strength. And, indeed, he was her strength when she lay in the hospital unable to help herself, but secure in the knowledge that her Bill would see that she was cared for. Now Bill is alone, but there is always the shadow of Ruth with him, waiting for him to join her once again.

Tom and Barbara were married during World War II just before he was sent to the Pacific. They hardly had time to get to know each other before he was gone. Their bonding during the next two years was done by correspondence. When he returned as a hero, they were able to pick up the pieces of their marriage rather quickly because they had written to each other their innermost thoughts and feelings unreservedly. In some ways they may have gotten to know each other better in that length of time than if they had been together. Each was able to read and re-read the thoughts of the other and feel a true bonding of spirits.

I saw Barbara the other day after many years. She told me that Tom is the victim of Alzheimer's disease and is becoming more and more difficult to manage. I asked if she would institutionalize him and was instantly sorry that the words had passed my lips. She said, "I don't know what tomorrow will bring. I am living one day at a time. I know that if the situation were reversed, he would care for me as long as possible. When he is so unreasonable and difficult, I find a few moments to be alone and read again the letters that he wrote to me during the war. It stirs my memory and reminds me of how he used to be, how he loved me, and what a caring person he was. We have been through so much together, and throughout our marriage, we cherished the love that drew us together in the beginning. I'm so thankful for those memories."

John and Alice had a wonderful celebration on their fiftieth wedding anniversary. Their children gave them a trip around the world and they set off with great excitement, promising pictures and slides to show when they returned. They lapsed quickly back to their carefree, childless, early years of marriage. They delighted in each other and enjoyed revived sexual pleasures. Life was good and fun, and each new city was theirs to explore as if no one had discovered its treasures before.

It was with mixed emotions that they arrived in London as the last stop before returning home. They hated to see this idyllic time come to an end but they were also looking forward to seeing children and friends again. This was when Alice noticed the little knot or lump in her breast. All of a sudden it was there. She put it out of her mind and didn't mention it to John. Why upset him? He had always been unable to cope when she had the slightest ailment.

After they had been home for a couple of weeks, Alice went to the doctor and had her check the lump. Within days, Alice underwent radical surgery, followed by chemotherapy. Now after six years, Alice's body is riddled with cancer. She is very courageous and friends enjoy visiting when she feels able to see them. One is always impressed with the warmth that is so genuine between John and Alice as he cares for her. He considers it a privilege to be the one who can do things for her to make her as comfortable as possible. He, no doubt, feels cheated that the best thing in his life is slipping away, but he is not missing the opportunity to give Alice what she needs. He is committed to loving and caring for her to the very end.

That is what true love is ... committed love. It is the passionate, desiring love that has developed into respect and caring. Mature love realizes that respect, good memories, care, and commitment all add up to a love that lasts and makes life beautiful.

For You to Do

Ask yourself these questions:

1. Have you known each other long enough to know each other well?
2. Have you seen each other in many circumstances? With your family and friends? In your normal family settings?
3. Are you able to disagree and be reconciled without the same one always having to "give in"?
4. When you are apart, do you miss each other? Is there pain in separation?
5. Are you proud of your fiancé(e)?
6. Are you good friends and well on your way to being best friends?
7. Does your relationship renew your strength or does it drain and tire you?
8. Can you mutually enjoy each other without the constant need for physical expression?
9. Are you planning on your love to change your partner after marriage?
10. Can you be honest with your fiancé(e)? If so, do you feel that he/she is honest with you?

4

Who Are You?

Paul Tournier, the renowned Swiss psychotherapist, tells of being in a solemn worship service in a Geneva cathedral. In the large gathering was a man who had brought his pre-school son. As the preacher began to speak, the child looked up in amazement and clearly, in the hushed silence of the nave, said, "Daddy, who is that man talking up there?" I would suspect that all of us feel like asking that question about ourselves: "Who is that person up there?" How can we discover the true person bottled up inside all the facades?

The fact is that you could remain hidden from yourself and from others all your life by assuming that you aren't worth knowing about. What an awful way to feel about oneself! Actually, what that says is that you are a selfish person who hates himself. The self-hater is one who is sensitive and domineering, demanding that other people feed his ego. Another type of self-hater is the one who will very quickly tell you how humble and misunderstood he is. He feels mistreated by society because he cannot love himself.

The Need for Self-Worth

When you see a person who proclaims that "he doesn't count," or that "he isn't worth anything," pray sincerely that he will learn to value himself. A person must learn to do good for himself in order to fulfill God's purpose in his life and in order to love another person.

The way we feel about ourselves determines to a great extent how we appear to other people. When you see someone who is slopping around in a bedraggled bathrobe or dress, with uncombed hair and a cigarette hanging from her lips, you can be sure that she is suffering from severe self-hate. The extent to which we love ourselves determines whether we eat right, get enough sleep, don't smoke, wear seat belts, exercise, dress appropriately, and so on. Each of these choices is really a statement of how much one cares about living.

As you can see, much of the sickness that one incurs could be eliminated or modified greatly by taking good care of oneself. It is important to both mental and physical health to feel pride in yourself. Self-esteem and self-love are not sinful, but make life worth living. Studies show that the body responds to the messages that we send. They may be "live" or "die" messages. A growing self-esteem and a conscious effort to develop optimistic attitudes will impact your physical health and also the health of your marital relationship.

What can one do about changing a self-destructive person into a self-accepting, caring individual who can relate in a healthy way to others? First, he has to learn to love and appreciate himself. This may require professional counseling or it may be possible for him to progress by coming to terms with the fact that we humans are made in the image of God and that He loves us unconditionally. That makes it perfectly all right for us to love ourselves.

Don't forget the admonition "to love your neighbor as yourself." That tells us that we first have to love ourselves. Then we have to practice this admonition to love both ourselves and others. It isn't always easy, because no one is lovable all the time. However, it is up to each of us not to be a difficult person to love. Don't be a joy-killer or a dream-stealer.

Who Am I?

So now we are back to the question, "Who am I?" Our view of ourselves is vital to our ability to relate in a healthy, intimate way to another person. We need a firm sense of personal identity, of who we are as separate individuals. Each person needs to have discovered this in adolescence. One reason that so many teenage marriages fail is that they cut short the time needed to establish a strong self-identity.

People who have developed a healthy self-image are much more likely to be able to relate maturely to another person. Healthy self-esteem allows one to be unselfish and thus to achieve intimacy in the relationship. A person who has a weak self-image will often cope with this by moving away from other people and also from himself. The person who has difficulty in relating intimately with another person also has difficulty relating to himself. The big step is to think well of yourself and then to be willing to be open to others. We must also realize that this healthy self-esteem is not a once-and-for-all achievement. It is an ongoing need. There are times in life when things go badly or when there is a crisis that shakes even the healthiest self-esteem. Each stage of life brings its problems, joys, and changes. Our personal well-being hinges on our ability to grow and creatively develop self-worth.

Healthy self-esteem ensures that you are going to grow in every area of life and that you will not stagnate into a green pond of despondency, dragging down everyone near you. Healthy self-esteem is a quiet sense of self-respect, a feeling of self-worth. Healthy self-esteem means that you are glad to be YOU!

College Romance

Liz was my college friend. She was tall, slender, and had a wonderful sense of humor. She was what I now call "a really good" person, always making sure that everyone around her was happy and satisfied. As she was growing up in a small town in north Georgia, her whole life centered around family and church and the status quo. She always wanted to be a cheerleader, but was afraid of entering the competition. She wanted to go to parties, but was afraid to admit that she didn't know how to dance. She decided that the easiest way to face life was to join the ranks of the women in her family and community who believed that women were meant to care for others, especially for men.

Liz was so pretty that as soon as she arrived on campus, one of the star football players claimed her as "his" property and she became Bob's girl. He directed her choice of classes, clothes, friends, everything. They dated for about two years and when Bob graduated, they got married. Never mind that she might never be able to finish college. Bob was in control.

I lost track of Liz for a while and at a twenty-year college reunion, I was happy to see that she seemed to be a happy, well-adjusted person. I noted that she was still very pretty and well-dressed. Bob was attentive but not possessive as he had been in the early years, and I remarked to Liz how different she seemed to be. She told me that life had been very difficult for them in the early years of marriage. They had two children before their third anniversary and Bob had had difficulty in business ventures. They moved frequently to avoid facing difficult situations and also in hopes that a move would help their wounded marriage. They almost reached the point of divorce but agreed to try marriage counseling.

They were surprised to learn that both of them had severe self-esteem problems. She learned that she was perfectly capable of making decisions on her own. He found out that he could profit from the friendship and cooperation of an "equal partner" relationship. Now each of them had become secure in themselves. She was free to think and he was free to be himself and not an eternal "superman."

It takes two healthy individuals to make a happy, healthy marriage. As the years go by, you will shape and be shaped by your partner, but never to the point of sacrificing your own individual personhood.

For You to Do

1. Look at the following limited definitions. Apply them to your own life and then discuss them with your fiancé(e). How will these three psychological forces affect your life as a couple?
   PRIDE (Unrealistic appraisal): Superior to others
   LOW ESTEEM (Unrealistic appraisal): Inferior to others
   HEALTHY SELF-ESTEEM (Realistic appraisal): Equal to others
2. Think about the following questions and answer them honestly.

   a. What do I like about myself?

   b. What do I dislike about myself?

   c. Do I like being a woman/man?

   d. Do I feel that I am a worthwhile person in myself, or do I need to be needed in order to justify my existence?

   e. Can I be alone, but not lonely?

   f. I enjoy meeting new people and experiencing new things (yes, no)

5

Where Are You Coming From?

Nobody understands why we choose one person to love and not another. Our degree of maturity, the way we feel about our parent of the opposite sex, or any number of complicated reasons go into the process of "falling in love." It is definitely true that people carry influences from the past into their marriages, and they spread into every nook and cranny of our lives.

We get our ideas of how men and women should act in marriage from observing our parents and the roles they filled for each other. We decide that we like or dislike the way our parents related to each other and vow that we will be different. For example, a domineering, addictive father and a helpless, cowering mother set up a pattern that is difficult to avoid in a child's adult life and marriage. Or perhaps it is the powerful, dogmatic mother and a weak, spineless father that is the example. Parents do not understand the extent of the influence of their relationship on generations to come!

The Family Factor

The way we relate to other people is also shaped by the way our families approached the outside world. Perhaps your family was very stoic, never showing any emotion to the family or to others. This can create an inability to be intimate in the marriage relationship. Parents who close themselves off from each other and their children make it difficult for their adult children to develop meaningful relationships. If a person from this type of family marries a person from an open, loving, caring family, the shock may create problems. It may require professional counseling to overcome it.

Our self-image comes directly from what our parents think of themselves and of their children. Parents who are insecure about themselves usually instill a similar sense of insecurity in their children. Parents who constantly criticize and disapprove make their children feel unworthy and unlovely. However, just the opposite is also true. Parents who feel good about themselves are able to affirm and support their children emotionally.

If the love that parents exhibit to their children comes with strings attached, then the child's self-image becomes distorted. The same problem surfaces if parental love allows total indulgence. This makes for a weak and dependent adult. It may also make the child react in confusion and anger at the slightest frustration.

Some parents are so immature and spoiled that their children become their parents. I have a friend who says that her parents were so immature and selfish that they depended on her to parent them. They ran to her with their marital problems and their emotional needs. It has made it difficult for her to make a commitment to a serious relationship.

In the worst marital situations, one partner abuses the other to make up for deep-felt inadequacies or the hurts of long ago. Too often a spouse bears the brunt of long pent-up anger because it seems all right to abuse a spouse, but not to confront parents.

Brothers and sisters also have an effect on the marriage relationship. Such things as whether a girl has an older brother(s) or a boy has an older or younger sister(s) and whether the parents tried to maintain a traditional home or rear the children of both sexes as equals affect intimate, adult relationships.

Previous Marriages

Another ghost of the past that can have a serious impact on a present marriage are the children of a previous marriage and the

former spouse. Children are obvious proof of a former relationship, whether it was happy or terrible. Child support payments,
alimony, visiting rights, and other complications of divorce
affect the way a new couple copes with their relationship. A
former spouse, living or dead, has colored the expectations of
his/her past partner. These must be acknowledged and dealt
with.

Three Generations

Many family therapists say that marital relationships and
difficulties involve three generations: a couple, their children,
and both sets of parents. Many of our early family relationships
are very positive and greatly enhance the adult child's potential
for a successful marriage. When there is warmth, touching, and
affection shown openly in the home, it is easier for the child to
be open and loving as an adult. He or she learns to be generous
and caring for others. When parents can demonstrate the ability
to transcend their difficulties without disintegrating; when parents can teach coping skills by example, this is one of the greatest
gifts that can be given to children.

Now is the time to think about the ghosts in your past that
will influence your marriage. The biggest thing to remember is
that it is possible to change. Sometimes people will not try to
change because they fear the pain of change and also fear the
unknown. Changes can be wrenching, but they are usually
worth the effort. The depth of your relationship will more than
compensate for the pain. No one is ever too old to change.

Expectations and Adjustments

Maureen came to me in great distress because she was facing
a traumatic decision. She had fallen in love with a charming
young man who wanted her to marry him. The problem was
that he had been previously married right out of high school
and had two small children. His former wife and children lived
out of state and he made the trip once every month to visit

them. Since Maureen did not know Pete's former wife, she was afraid that she reminded Pete of her and that the same mistakes would occur again.

Maureen was wise to recognize one of the dangers in remarriage. I suggested that she and Pete spend some time with a marriage counselor to make sure that his self-esteem was in place and that he was not trying to marry a carbon copy of his first wife to prove that he can make it work. If Pete has grown emotionally and has learned from past failure, he may be a very good marriage partner. My last contact with Maureen was an invitation to their wedding. She had slipped a personal note in it for me. "I feel like we're ready for this step. We are both aware of the possible problems and are determined to discuss them openly and to seek help if one of us feels threatened. Thanks for the advice. I wouldn't want to miss out on marriage to Pete!"

Betty is a friend whose family is one of those wonderfully spontaneous, "huggy kissy" types who show great affection whenever anyone comes or goes. She was telling me about her two new daughters-in-law and their reactions to this emotionally demonstrative family. During the Christmas season there was a lot of coming and going, and new family faces to be greeted. One daughter-in-law always jumped up and almost literally stood in line to get her share of the hugging, while the other, though not unpleasant, tried to hide and avoid the passionate expressions of affection. Both are lovely and charming young women who dearly love their new family, but Nancy, having been brought up in a rather emotionless, undemonstrative family, was having a hard time giving and receiving so much "excess" warmth. Fortunately for Nancy, Betty understood what was going on and could be supportive and sensitive to Nancy's feelings. The time may come when Nancy will feel comfortable enough to be "huggy kissy," too.

Sometimes a person's birth order in the family has an impact on his or her reactions to new family developments. This was the case with Mary Jane. She was the fourth daughter with two younger brothers. In a family of six children and one moderate income, there was not much left over to indulge the desires of a young teenage girl. Mary Jane was always the recipient of the older sisters' hand-me-downs and rarely got to choose a new dress for herself. Imagine her excitement and surprise, and the pleasure of her new mother-in-law (who had no daughters), when their mutual needs came together! As long as Mary Jane doesn't become selfish and base her relationship with her new mother-in-law on what she can get, and as long as her mother-in-law doesn't overwhelm her and try to run her marriage, this could be a dream come true on both sides.

Many times our expectations of what a husband or wife should be like stem directly from our view of our own mother or father. I was surprised, for example, that my husband had no desire to go to the grocery store with me. My father nearly always went with my mother. On his part, Bill was shocked that I expected him to go with me.

My father made a production out of paying the bills each month. Everyone in the house knew what was going on and tried to avoid my father as he commandeered the dining room table. Imagine my shock when my new husband suggested that I be responsible for writing checks. Should I make a production out of it like my father? Sometimes I am tempted to do that in order to get a little sympathy!

People are funny, and family backgrounds make them even funnier! Blending backgrounds can sometimes be a traumatic experience. When in doubt about what is making you or your spouse "crazy," do a little digging into his/her background. It could save a lot of wear and tear on nerves!

For You to Do

Tell each other about these things:

1. Your family consisted of (name all persons who lived in your home). Other important people included (aunts, uncles, cousins, grandparents, etc.).
2. Tell each other about a significant event that included a large part of the family.
3. Was there much sickness in the family? If so, describe the effect it had on the family members.
4. Are you very close to your family? Do you feel that your fiancé(e) is too close to his/her family?
5. Who are some of the important people in your life (teachers, etc.)?

6. How did your family handle money? Can you recall some significant occasions when finances were a critical issue?
7. Tell some of the positive, wonderful things about your parents and family.
8. Tell some of the problem areas of your family. Are there alcohol or addiction problems, abusive behavior, etc.?
9. If one or both of you are reweds, be sure to discuss your child care arrangements, finances, the treatment of former spouses, and any other area of possible conflict.

6

Why Are You Getting Married?

It really is hard not to hold unrealistic expectations for your approaching marriage. Somehow we all believe in the ending of the fairy tale, "and they lived happily ever after." That phrase can certainly become true, but it will depend on your (and your spouse's) interpretation of the words. You may not realize that you are living "happily ever after" until many years later, when you take an opportunity to look back and evaluate life. A marriage built on fantasies or dreams is risky because it takes a firm foundation of commitment and trust to weather the storms that will blow against your world.

Reasons for Marriage

Why get married? There are many reasons people get married—some good, some bad. Let's look at a few and you can decide if any of these apply to you:

- To escape an unhappy home (alcoholic parent(s), molestation, unusually strict, etc.).
- In rebellion against parental influence and/or defiance of family traditions and values.
- With an unhealthy desire to be taken care of as the hidden agenda in the relationship. If this need to be cared for is shared, and strength from each is passed back and forth, intimacy can be nurtured. Otherwise, it can be deadly to the relationship.

- "It's time to get married." Social or family pressure, fear of being left out or waiting too long, may push a person into a hasty decision.
- Feeling sorry for a person. This does not mean that you should marry him or her. That person may make you feel guilty, but you should seek help to determine your true feelings.
- The desire to escape loneliness. No one wants to be lonely or spend the rest of their lives alone. However, being married and lonely is probably worse than being single and lonely.
- Pregnancy. Marriages under these circumstances have the possibility of being healthy, happy relationships, but they require even more attention than others. In about one-fourth of all marriages, the bride is pregnant.
- Comfort. Being comfortable with your spouse means being best friends. You can share joys, disappointments, beliefs, dreams, fears, all of life with your mate/friend, knowing that you can be yourself.
- Intimacy. In marriage we want emotional, physical, and aesthetic intimacy. We must be willing to knock down barricades that have been erected to protect vulnerable areas in our lives.
- The search for a parent substitute. A girl may seek someone who will protect her and care for her as her father did (or as she thought a father should). A man may be looking for a mother substitute, a wife who will understand that he really is still a little boy and who will see that his needs are met.
- A deep hunger for a permanent marriage relationship. Marriage provides the setting for each partner to grow and learn to face life with the help of a caring mate.
- A secret club for two. You share secrets, work, play, "hang out" together, and have fun together. You like each other more every day and the trust that grows keeps your friendship getting better and better.
- The need to be truly loved. Marriage is the natural setting in which to experience this type of intimate communion. To know that you are the most important person in your mate's life is an unspeakable joy.
- To fill out one's personality. I don't mean that one is not a whole person without a mate, but when one marries well, a new dimension is added to both personalities. Sometimes we need to be told by someone who really loves us that a certain attitude or idea is simply not right. When done in an appropriate way, we can benefit greatly from the opinions of our mate.

- Sexual fulfillment. This natural, pleasurable way of expressing total commitment and trust in each other is best enjoyed in the confines of marriage. Physical enjoyment of each other becomes a part of the fabric of your growing relationship.
- The need for a lasting friend. Committed love and friendship, mixed with caring, respect, and memories, will make life worth living.

Norma and George

My cousin is a good example of someone who married for the wrong reason. I never understood why Norma married George. I'll never forget the family crisis that erupted the weekend that she broke the news. My aunt and uncle had only one child and they had put all their energy, love, and work into Norma. The rest of the family was kept informed of all of her accomplishments and my mother was pressed into service as a seamstress to make sure that Norma had the best and most fashionable clothes for every occasion. I remember hearing whispered conversations about bank loans and second mortgages to make payments for college and the expensive sorority that was so vital to her happiness.

My aunt and uncle were devastated when Norma brought George home to meet the family and announced that they were getting married . . . and soon! I was an impressionable sixteen years old at the time and even though I relished the thoughts of a big wedding (which I knew would be forthcoming), I was concerned about Norma's choice.

George was a party animal from a nonreligious background, from another part of the country, with divorced parents. He talked as though he knew absolutely everything, except what he planned to do with his life. Norma would be expected to drop out of school; maybe someday she would be able to finish college. This was what got my attention. Norma and I had been brought up to believe that finishing college was virtually necessary to ensure entrance into heaven! I couldn't believe that she would take that risk, but I became a believer when, in a few months, I was a bridesmaid in a semi-happy wedding.

Within a few years, Norma had presented my aunt and uncle

with three grandchildren. There was a lot of traveling back and forth to take care of these babies. My aunt would roll her eyes toward heaven and loudly question George's sanity. He had changed jobs again and that meant another move. Now his latest idea was for Norma's parents to take care of his family so that Norma could go back to school to finish her education. Then she could teach school and help support him in the style he desired.

Finally, after almost twenty-two years of marriage, George decided that it was time to split. The time was perfect for him. They had just moved to Atlanta and had sold their home; the oldest girl had eloped with a man ten years her senior; and the middle child, a girl, was running with a drug-infested crowd. Only the son seemed normal. What a mess!

It turned out that Norma's life straightened out and her nerves settled after George made his exit. I still wondered why Norma married George. She finally answered me: "It seemed like a good idea at the time. He was a lot of fun on a date and a great dancer. School was so boring and marriage seemed like a good thing. Boy, did I learn the hard way!"

For You to Do

1. On a separate sheet of paper write down all the answers you can think of to the question, "Why do you want to get married?" Share your responses with each other.
2. Do you think that your fiancé(e) is the person with whom to share the rest of your life?
3. Do your parents, siblings, close friends approve of this marriage? If not, do you know why? Have you seriously considered the possibility that their reasoning may be something for you to heed?
4. Do you feel certain that you can trust your fiancé(e)? If you have any doubts, you should think about the reasons.

7

Are You Ready to Marry?

Martha was sixteen that summer. One warm evening she sat beside her dad on the back porch. After listening to the frogs singing for a while, she turned to him and asked, "Daddy, how do you know when you're in love? How does it make you feel?" He was taken by surprise at her question but set about the task of arranging his thoughts so that he could respond to her. Somehow he knew that this was a serious question.

"Well, Martha," he began, "love is a feeling, a warm glow deep down inside that makes you feel special. Love is making someone else feel special. It is sharing the good times and the bad times and knowing that your loved one understands. Love is a special caring for someone. . . ." His voice trailed off as he became lost in his own memories. Martha sighed and said, "I hope I'll know when it comes. I don't want to miss it."

Martha is right. You won't want to miss love. So how will you know when it's the real thing? It is easy when one is basking in the glow of romance to ignore the little nagging, tentative questions that you may have. But *now* is the time to work out any fears that may stalk your mind.

The Real Thing

Some people blame the steady increase in divorce on the fact that the excitement of romantic love and the idea of getting married keeps one or both partners from making intelligent evaluations of themselves and the life they may have together. Romance is a big part of the picture, but couples cannot become victims of romantic love. Life must be lived in reality. You may be "in love" with the idea of a wedding, and perhaps in the fairy tale lore of "living happily ever after."

Being engaged, planning a wedding, and making vital decisions about the future make one feel very grown up, very adult. It is almost as if the answer to the question, "What will you be when you grow up?" is, "Married." One partner may not desire to be an adult when he/she finds out how difficult it is on a daily basis.

One summer when we were on vacation, our youngest son had a friend with him. One evening we were having a rather serious conversation around the dinner table and both boys somewhat vehemently said that they did not want to grow up. They preferred to remain boys without the responsibilities of being grown men. They are both in their late twenties now; the friend is still desperately avoiding the responsibilities of being "grown up."

Are You Ready?

Are you ready to marry? It's wise to consider the financial situation of each person. It will not be a healthy start for the marriage if, as a couple, you have to depend on one or both sets of parents. This puts a strain on all the relationships. For a parent, it would be very difficult to have a "no strings attached" attitude toward a couple in this arrangement.

Jason and Beth had a "coast to coast" romance. He was stationed in the military on the west coast and met Beth while visiting friends in San Diego. They continued their romance long distance after he moved back to the east coast. Jason and Beth had a lovely California wedding and then he brought his bride home to Atlanta. Jason was well-educated, from a wealthy family. He was given a good job and all seemed to be going well. The problem was that Jason did not like to get up and go to work at a specified time in the morning. He could not see any reason for punctuality. Needless to say, the company he worked for fired him.

This became a pattern for Jason. In the meantime, Beth had one child and was expecting the second. Jason's parents finally agreed to set him up in a little business that he could run at his leisure and supplemented his earnings with an allowance and the proceeds from a trust fund his grandmother had left him. Jason's mother felt that since they were funding them, she had the right to choose their groceries. As a friend and neighbor, I got to hear all the complaints from Beth about the interference of Jason's parents. After twenty years it still hasn't changed. If only Beth had asked herself, "Am I ready to marry?" If only she had known more about Jason, a lot of heartache could have been avoided . . . or at least anticipated.

Often it is beneficial to both parent and child to give a new couple money for a down payment on a house, or, in case of emergency, to offer a loan or a gift of money. Each family has to decide what is appropriate.

Are you financially stable enough for marriage? Don't forget that two really cannot live as cheaply as one. If this is a second marriage, finances will be an especially important factor. When there are children from a previous marriage to support financially and emotionally, both partners should agree on financial matters. Nothing should be hidden, because it could place a hardship on the marriage.

Other Considerations

Are you ready to marry? Do either of you have a health problem? How would this affect your life together? Health problems should be openly discussed. The marriage relationship does best when two healthy people (body, mind, and emotions) come together. A person who majors in complaining about poor health may be sending a signal that there are other problems to be explored.

Sometimes both men and women avoid dealing with reality or facing personal confrontation by becoming sick. Remember the child who could always throw up when faced with a school crisis? Or your friend's mother who always got a sick headache when something went wrong? Have you and your fiancé(e) learned to deal with reality in an appropriate way?

Are you ready to marry? Or is it that your biological clock is ticking ominously? Age is a factor in the timing of some marriages. Women especially feel that time is pushing them if motherhood is a primary goal.

Are you ready to marry? Have you tried to discern God's will in this matter? Since this is the most important decision you will make, it is imperative to sense God's will in the choice of your mate as well as the timing of your marriage. A sense of well-being, of feeling good deep down inside when you take time to think and pray through this matter, will give you confidence in God's intense interest in your life.

It is important not to rush impulsively into marriage, but it is equally important not to put it off if you're both ready. Life is too short to miss the opportunity to begin building your relationship and making memories.

For You to Do

1. List on paper the reasons you should marry now. Share them with your fiancé(e).
2. List some reasons you are marrying your fiancé(e). Why do you love him/her? Share your lists with each other.

8

Breaking an Engagement

By now you have probably come to the conclusion that being engaged is a lot more involved than you had expected it to be! Being engaged sounds so romantic. It is exciting to choose rings and to make wedding plans. However, the most important thing you can do now is to examine your relationship, talk openly about the issues raised in the previous chapters, and decide if the next step, marriage, is for you.

The following chapters will help you talk about family relationships, money, and careers. It will be no disgrace if you come to the conclusion that marriage is not for you at this time. It is much easier to break an engagement than to get a divorce or maintain a miserable marriage.

Broken Relationships

Janet and Dan came to our class for engaged couples several years ago. Dan was in his early forties and had two teenage children by a previous marriage. Janet was in her mid-thirties and had never been married. She was a pretty young woman but had always had a weight problem and very few boyfriends. She was thrilled to be getting married and could hardly wait for the wedding day to arrive.

Dan, on the other hand, seemed a reluctant groom, very reticent and quiet. After one of the sessions on finances, in which we discussed quite frankly the problems of money when there is child support or alimony to be paid, we noticed that they left very quickly. They did not come to the next few sessions and I called Janet to see what was going on.

She was heartbroken and a little angry. It seems that after the discussion on finances, Dan had decided that he could not handle any more responsibility, even with two incomes. They had agreed to continue seeing each other but without planning a wedding anytime soon. That is a sad story, but it was fortunate that they determined before marriage that he was frightened. In the end, the money situation turned out to be his excuse for escaping the relationship.

John and Sue came to our Newlywed seminar about two months after their marriage. From the beginning, the faculty and I wondered why these two had gotten married. These were two people who had been determined to marry regardless of what family or friends said. They each came to the seminar hoping that the group would confirm their individual viewpoint on everything. They agreed on absolutely nothing and we were all afraid that one would kill the other before the next session.

It did nearly come to that. They were constantly abusing each other, and his physical abuse finally got to the point that she had to leave and threaten to have him arrested. Before they had been married six months, John and Sue were facing each other in divorce court. The agony and frustration that they experienced could have been avoided if they had taken time to get to know each other better with supervised help. The bitterness over the division of wedding gifts and the accusations of the families were devastating.

Don't be afraid or ashamed to break your engagement or to postpone the wedding until your feelings are certain. It is normal to experience a few anxious moments and some self-doubt; after all, you'll be spending the rest of your life with this person and what he/she becomes determines to a great extent what you also become. It is a risk, but there is no gain without risk.

Postponement Strategies

If you agree to break your engagement, we offer these suggested guidelines:

- Seek further counseling.
- Don't prolong the decision. The longer you wait, the harder it will be.
- Do not intimidate or try to manipulate your fiancé(e).
- Be honest and willing to communicate.
- Allow yourself to grieve.
- Do not rush immediately into a new relationship. Allow time to recover.
- Remember that it is better to break an engagement than to break up a marriage.

For You to Do

Review the following situations or statements and think about them as they may relate to your marriage. Honestly share your answers with each other.

1. I (do, do not) feel accepted by my future spouse's family.
2. I (will, will not) have difficulty leaving my parents and making my spouse my first responsibility.
3. I (can, cannot) live on a budget. I (can, cannot) manage my finances well.
4. I (know, do not know) about my future spouse's religion.
5. I (do, do not) want to have children. I (do, do not) feel comfortable talking about this.
6. I am (aware, not aware) of birth control methods.
7. I (could, could not) handle prolonged illness in myself or my spouse.
8. Our marriage would survive if the wife had greater career opportunities and earned more money. (yes, no)
9. Our marriage could survive a major relocation. (yes, no)
10. Our marriage could survive unfaithfulness on the part of either spouse. (yes, no)
11. I care more and more about my fiancé(e) and feel cared for in return. (yes, no)
12. Even though one out of two marriages fail, ours will be the one that makes it. (yes, no)

PART II

Marriage Secured (Preparing for the Future)

9

Money and My Background

Money is the leading cause of arguments and misunderstandings in married couples. Newlyweds are not alone in this problem. Many times couples who have been married thirty years or more still haven't been able to solve their financial situation satisfactorily. Rich or poor, or somewhere in between, there are multiple money issues to be decided.

Each partner comes to the marriage with different attitudes about money. Your spending habits, financial backgrounds, desires for life-style and social status can lead to great frustration, heated arguments, and hurt feelings. It is important to explore your attitudes, desires, and needs as well as your backgrounds concerning financial matters. This chapter and the following three chapters will help you to become aware of your own as well as your fiancé(e)'s expectations. It is important not to gloss over this issue because, most likely, it will become a battleground if some significant money management decisions are not made early.

These decisions may change as time progresses because your financial status and life-style may change. Flexibility within certain parameters will be important as you mature.

Parents do not think of their children as adults until they are making and managing their money and/or get married. It is helpful when the former precedes the latter. Being dependent on parents financially keeps you open to their well-intentioned interference. It is difficult to become financially independent; it takes time and a lot of communication.

Money Memories

Now think about your own childhood.

If you are from a broken home, your finances may have been marginal. Single parent families are the new poor in our culture. You may not be from a single parent family but still have been relatively deprived financially. This does not discredit your background, but simply indicates that your view of handling money will be different from one who is from a moderate to wealthy home.

If your family was/is wealthy, you have an entirely different view of money. Wealth is generally thought of as the solution to most problems; however, the rich have problems with drug and alcohol abuse, health, family quarrels, and divorce, just like the poor. You or your family may have felt "used" by so-called friends who saw you only as a donor to their projects. You may also wonder if your fiancé(e) is marrying you for your money. The wealthy have a great responsibility to learn to manage well what God has given them. You must understand yourself and your wealth in order to be a healthy, well-balanced person.

If your family is moderately well-off financially, you still have to understand how your financial background will affect you as you set up your own household. In this wide range of "average," there are numerous ways that families deal with finances. In over half of all two-parent families, the wife and mother will work at least part-time during some stage of the marriage. The way your parents handled money, the division of chores, the arguments or silences, made an impression on you that will surface in your own marriage.

The Dining Room Table

We had an interesting arrangement for finances in my family. As I look back on it now, I realize that my father's self-esteem was directly related to his ability to provide for his family. During the thirties, almost everyone had a difficult time making ends meet and my father was providing for two families. My grandmother and her daughter's family depended on some financial help from my father each month in order to pay the rent on their house. As I mentioned earlier, each payday my father would spread out the checkbook and all the bills on the dining room table; we learned to tiptoe around him. He would demand an accounting for each item on each bill, and it was a thoroughly harrowing experience. I can see now that the dining room table was his place of operation because it was the center of the house. No matter where you were going in the house, you had to pass through the war zone. There was no doubt as to who was in charge of the money at our house. I never knew how poor we were. I did know that we were not rich. We never lacked for anything, but I always worried a little. I just assumed that every family had similar scenes at least once a month.

Imagine my surprise when Bill and I married and he showed no interest in managing the household accounts. I taught school while he finished his seminary education, so there wasn't much to manage. It was a frightening experience for me to realize that I would be the one to write the checks and balance the checkbook. Bill has become an astute businessman and understands all about large budgets of great churches. He has planned well for our future, but I still make sure the bills are paid and we're not overdrawn at the bank.

Marital Adjustments

We had a lot of adjusting to do in our early years concerning finances because of our opposite attitudes about money. Bill worked on the premise that money is to spend and enjoy. My idea was that money has to be judiciously spent and that "a penny saved is a penny earned." I certainly couldn't argue with his generous spirit because I benefited greatly from it. Through a lot of talking and experimenting, we have both matured in our attitudes about money and have also learned to handle our finances more carefully. It probably worked out pretty well that we were opposites in this matter. If we had both been generous to a fault, we'd be in the poorhouse. But if we had both been like me, we would never have been free from the tyranny of stinginess. I now realize that my father was really a very generous man in ways that I did not recognize at the time. I'm glad that I have learned the lesson of being in control of our money, not allowing our money to be in control of us.

For You to Do

The following questions are meant to help you uncover latent fears, unexplained desires, hurt feelings or comfortable feelings, and attitudes about money. We need to deal with the fact that, right or wrong, our society equates a person's wealth (or lack of it) with the person himself/herself. Self-esteem often comes wrapped in paper money!

After answering the following questions, share them with your fiancé(e).

Remember how your family handled money.

1. When you were growing up, did you receive an allowance? As payment for certain chores? For just existing?
2. Were you punished by having your allowance taken away?
3. Did you save money for special purchases? Remember some specifically.
4. Who controlled the checkbook?
5. Did you always feel secure that there would be money for whatever you needed?
6. Were you afraid that there would not be funds available for college or other training?
7. Have your parents always bailed you out of money troubles?
8. Do you feel that financial security is very important and want to have a lot of money?
9. Were your parents generous or stingy?
10. Did you learn to tithe by seeing the example of your parents?

After thinking about your financial background, talk to your fiancé(e) about the way your parents handled money. Neither of you should make any judgment on the other's family but use this exchange as a way to get a clear picture of the other's past experiences.

10

Money and Where I Am Now

Whether we like it or not, we are all prone to measure a person's worth by his wealth and possessions. To have the proper view of money is of vital importance in our relationships to others. John Wesley, eighteenth-century spiritual giant and founder of the Methodist church, had a wonderful philosophy concerning money. "Gain all you can. Save all you can. Give all you can." He believed that people should earn as much money as they are capable of earning, save as much as possible, and give as much as possible to worthy causes.

There are two basic perspectives on money. One is based on greed and the other on generosity. It is important to explore your own perspective on this subject. You may be surprised at some hidden feelings and attitudes. This is the time to evaluate your philosophy of money. It will help your marriage relationship to be much healthier and will alleviate some financial misunderstandings.

Trust and Independence

Money is a symbol of trust and security to most people. That is not bad in itself, but it can put a great deal of pressure on a marriage, especially in the early years. I know a young man who was terror-stricken when a department store offered him and his new wife a joint charge account. He imagined that she would charge excessively and he would be held accountable. It all boiled down to the fact that money (and his ability to earn it) was an intimate extension of himself. Money was evidence of his power and independence, and he was deathly afraid to let his wife touch this area of his life.

It is also possible that this man had been let down by someone, either financially or emotionally, and he wasn't ready to trust his wife yet. He had become used to relying on himself and this new sharing was a difficult adjustment. It will be very important that this man and his wife learn to trust and be trustworthy so that neither one will be emotionally or financially depleted or exploited. If this is a potential problem for you, share this feeling with your fiancé(e) in a loving, non-accusatory way so that you can work through it.

Control and Dependence

The question of who is in charge of the finances is a potentially explosive issue in most marriages. This is true in both traditional (husband as breadwinner) and partnership (two careers, mutual agreement roles) marriages. Money and sex are the two most powerful tools for control. Sometimes the mate who tries to control the finances seems to be doing so out of love and concern, or the fact that he or she has the better financial skills. However, underneath this is the fear that he/she will become powerless. Money is a measure of control. Even in marriages where money should be no problem, there is often anger and indignation when one or the other partner assumes that he/she can tell the other what to do. This is especially true with couples who have grown up in homes where the children were given a lot of responsibility and autonomy, or where one or both have been working and managing their own money for a long time.

This also includes the idea of how dependent or independent you each want to be in regard to money. It is usually a good idea for both husband and wife to be involved in planning and managing the finances. Impoverished people fight for survival, but in middle class homes, fights about money are often really fights about who makes the big decisions and who controls the direction the family moves in. Often one partner who is more aggressive and opinionated than the other will automatically become the decision-maker.

However, there is a balance of power that must be approved by both. For almost everyone, male or female, there is at times a temptation to be dependent. This, if allowed to continue, will shortchange both parties. One who is totally dependent is being prevented from gaining the self-confidence and skills needed to share in the responsibilities of marriage. If only one earns a paycheck, there should be some distribution of financial responsibilities, so that both can see the marriage as an adult partnership.

Budget Tyranny

Laura came to see our church counselor in great distress. It seems that her husband, Tom, traveled all week. When he returned home on Fridays, he demanded an accounting of every penny he had left for her and the children. If an emergency came up while he was away, she could not write a check until he had approved the expenditure. She had decided that even though Tom did not approve of the idea, she must get at least a part-time job so that she could have a little money to call her own.

The counselor insisted that Tom come in with Laura to talk about this situation. He reluctantly agreed. It took a lot of sessions for Tom to finally understand that the money he earned was really the money of the family and that instead of being the good provider he considered himself, he was actually depriving the family of things they needed and of the feeling of family trust. Tom had to learn that Laura could be trusted with "his" hard-earned money and that their relationship would improve immensely when Laura gained self-esteem in the knowledge that Tom trusted her.

Laura needed to feel like a partner in their relationship, not like a child. He finally understood that it was important for her to have a part-time job to buy a few special things without accounting to him. This situation took a long time to work out, but neither Tom nor Laura wanted to end the marriage and both were cooperative and willing to change. It would have saved a lot of heartache if they had communicated about finances before their marriage.

Traditionally, men have seen it as their role to provide for their wives, and women traditionally sought men who could offer stability, safety, and security. The idea of being supported by the husband was the equivalent of being loved. Even today when both spouses bring home a paycheck, in most marriages money is still seen as a sign of nurturance. Providing money for one's mate is a way of demonstrating affection and showing support. Many arguments about money are really expressing the frustration of one or both that they do not feel loved and cared for.

After you are married, you will need to look at this dependent/independent situation as it applies to you. This subject (money) will always require open communication. Your attitudes about money, caring, and nurturing will need to be examined often. Try to reach compromises to bridge your differences; don't necessarily try to change each other.

For You to Do

1. Together write down:

    a. How much money you each earn.
    b. What assets you each have.
    c. Loans or outstanding debts for each.
    d. What investments you have.
    e. Whether you can live on a budget.

2. How important is it to each of you to have a lot of money?
3. Is it important to have a luxurious life-style?
4. How do you feel about pooling money?
5. Do you insist on your own personal financial accounts?
6. How would you react if your fiancé(e) lost his job?
7. Are you generous with each other now?
8. Do you tithe to your church? Talk to each other about this.
9. Are you a skinflint or a big spender?
10. Are you able to act as an adult about money matters? Are you disciplined in this area?

11

Money and Our Blended Family

This topic, "Money and Our Blended Family," is becoming more and more important as so many people remarry. I believe that money will be a constant source of conflict in most of the new blended family units. Because money is one of the two major battles of a divorce (child custody is the other), the battlefield is left strewn with unexploded land mines. This is treacherous territory for a new spouse. It may be so frightening that he or she may choose not to marry into the situation.

In this chapter we are going to look at a few of the potential land mines involved with blended families. We do not intend to frighten anyone, but it is only fair for all concerned to understand the problem areas. Some things will be unchangeable until the children are grown and away from home.

Financial Reality

The first thing to understand is that you must face financial reality. Don't try to cover up the facts of how much money is or is not available. Basically, only a wealthy person can really afford to maintain two homes.

When a widow thinks of remarriage, she may have to decide whether the relationship is worth the price of losing some financial benefits that will cease when she remarries. If she is young and has young children, this may put a severe strain on the relationship. Her new husband may feel under great pres-

sure to make her happy and the children satisfied. There is also
a tendency to deify the dead spouse, forgetting that he or she
was in fact very human. Be sure you date long enough to work
through these feelings, and be sure that you can marry without
saying "look what I gave up" to your new spouse.

A Poor Gamble

Becky's husband had died when he was thirty-six, leaving
her with a four-year-old son to care for. Jeff had left his estate in
good condition and Becky could live satisfactorily on the
monthly payments she received from the trust fund and from
the government.

Three or four years after Jeff's death, Becky began to think
seriously about getting married again. She had been dating
several different men. One was always out of work and rather
unpolished. We couldn't understand why Becky even dated
him at all. He was always there, and she seemed to think that
she could take this raw material and make him over. The
problem was that when she remarried, the government supple-
ment would stop and could never be reinstated. All of Becky's
friends were opposed to the marriage and aghast that she would
gamble on the loss of income in light of this man's inability to
keep a job.

Becky married this man and has tried valiantly to make
something out of him. Sad to say, she is the one who is now the
breadwinner while he watches television and goes to job
interviews that never amount to anything. They have had to
borrow against the child's trust fund and college trust. Becky
threatens to throw him out of her house, but a promise from
him to do better and get a job always keeps her working for him.

Child Support

A divorced woman in a new marriage may soon realize that
one thing is still the same . . . money. Now it is further
complicated by remarriage. In a few instances, alimony is still
granted to a woman, but usually it is in the form of child

support. Alimony will stop once she remarries, but the child support will continue. The father of the children is responsible for his share of their support but we all know cases where payments are almost impossible to collect.

If the new spouse is a divorced father who has to pay child support, several scenarios can develop. If his new wife's children live with them and they do not receive support money, he will end up having to care for both families. This can be the legitimate source of great anger and frustration on the part of the adults involved. Unless he is quite wealthy, the financial drain will be tremendous. If the wife isn't already working, she will surely have to do so.

A woman who marries a man making child support payments must be aware that it will be difficult not to resent the monthly outgo. It can get depressing as time goes on, especially if the relationship is not rewarding or if she resents having to work while the former spouse makes demands.

It may also be some time before the new couple can afford a home if, as in many cases, the ex-wife got the house in the property settlement. All of these situations can threaten a new marriage unless the lines of communication are kept open.

Barry and Elaine look like the ideal couple. Both are tall, slender, and good-looking. Barry is always pleasant with a good word for everyone. Elaine is also a happy person except for once a month, when Barry writes the child support check for his son out of their joint account.

Elaine feels as if HER money is going to Barry's former spouse (even though it is labeled child support). Barry and Elaine felt it was important for them to pool their resources and operate out of one account to reinforce their unity as a family and their trust in each other. Now they are considering opening a special account for Barry to use specifically for child support. That way Elaine won't have to see the check and she'll not have a monthly attack of resentment. Fortunately, Elaine felt that she could openly discuss her feeling with Barry and he offered to make this change.

Money management is even more crucial in blended families because of the unusual circumstances. Be open about the situation; don't cover up the facts, unpleasant or not. No one likes unhappy surprises.

For You to Do

1. Share these facts with your partner:
   a. I have ____ (number of) children.
   b. I am financially responsible for: (details about monthly payments plus any other incidentals such as doctor, dental, etc.).
   c. These children (will, will not) live with us.
   d. My visitation rights are as follows:
   e. I own my own home and am financially able to make the payments. (yes, no)
   f. We will need two incomes to meet the financial requirements of our combined families. (yes, no)
   g. Generally speaking, this much money will be required to meet our monthly commitments: $_____

2. Discuss the possible emotional strain that financial commitments to an ex-spouse and/or children can create for your new family unit.
3. As soon as you marry, change your will to accommodate your new status. You owe this to your children and your new spouse. Both husband and wife must do this.
4. Promise that you will discuss your financial situation openly, honestly, and without hostility in order to keep debts from accumulating.
5. Seek professional help for both financial and emotional stress before problems become insurmountable.

12

Setting Budget Goals

No matter what you have heard, two cannot live as cheaply as one. You can safely assume that two can live as cheaply as two, and if you are lucky enough to find that by combining some things, you come out with a little extra money, congratulate yourselves on being so prudent!

In these days of unpredictable taxes, inflation, interest rates, and the breakdown of even new appliances and cars, it is ever more difficult to make ends meet. It will take several years together for you to work out a budget that meets your financial requirements. Even though your budget will change frequently in the first few years, it is imperative that you work through this sensitive issue in a nonthreatening way. This is true if you are a dual career couple or one works full time at home.

Wants and Needs

You must both be sensitive to the way you are spending money. What you WANT and what you NEED may be two different things and that must be reconciled. Deciding what is a luxury and what is a necessity must be determined by both of you. Not deciding can lead to more arguments. Both budgeting and spending money are ways of demonstrating power. In a well-balanced partnership marriage, both husband and wife should exercise this power jointly.

The question of life-style must also be faced squarely. You

must now establish financial goals in order to have the kind of home, neighborhood, school, vacations, and careers that you desire. Dreams are absolutely necessary, but they require realistic plans to reach them.

The number one battle topic of newlyweds is money. Very likely it will remain the biggest issue of debate for the entire marriage. Over eighty percent of the couples seeking divorce have unresolved conflicts over money. It is essential that you face this marriage-breaker head-on.

The Money God

Both husband and wife need to understand that if money becomes your god, then you are the slave and can never be satisfied. Jesus understood this and spoke more about money than anything else! Twenty centuries later, men are still lusting for it, dying for it, killing and being killed for it, and literally going to hell for it. Money has destroyed friendships, families, and marriages. The "world's" view of money leads us to measure a person's worth by what they have. We should be in control of our money, not the other way around. There is an old saying: "That which you own will eventually own you."

One of the ways that you can get in control of your money is to determine to follow the laws of God concerning tithing and generosity. The Old Testament makes it very clear that a tithe, one-tenth of your income, must be given to the storehouse (synagogue, church). God even invites us to test Him to see if He will not pour out blessings on those who follow this law. The New Testament upholds this precept through the teachings and illustrations of Jesus.

Many couples find this hard to do because they feel that there are other things they should do with the money that belongs to God. But there is never a better time to begin tithing than in the first years of marriage. It never gets easier. Would you like God to postpone His blessing on you and your family until "later"? If we want the blessings of God, we must be obedient.

There are some things about money and its management that need to be repeated over and over. Remember that money will not solve all of life's problems. Keep in mind that our society may say that the purpose of life is to make money, but that should not be the way it is. If it is, money will control your entire life and create more problems. Money should not be the controlling factor in your relationship. Money is a good servant but a terrible master. "If I had more money, my problems would be solved and I would be happy." The response to that statement is, "If you had more money, you would need more money. There is never enough to satisfy greed."

Debt Control

Compound interest is the eighth wonder of the world. Debt is compound interest in reverse. A budget will help you get or stay out of debt. There are many advantages of having a budget: (1) It will help you control your spending and anticipate your outgo. (2) It will help you to choose a standard of living. (3) It will help you to provide for your future, for your wants, and for investments. (4) A budget shows what your fixed expenses are. You have no control over your mortgage, rent, insurance, tithe, etc. (5) It also exposes your flexible expenses. You can control the amount you spend on clothing, travel, groceries, luxuries, etc.

The person who controls the purse strings sometimes feels very powerful. However, if the couple has honestly and cooperatively participated in the budget planning, it won't really matter who actually writes the checks. In a partnership, the person who has the skill and the time should be responsible for managing the expenses and paying the bills on time.

Many couples today are trying to keep separate checking accounts and divide the expenses equally. Some may be able to do this, but we have noted that within a year or two, they decide to combine accounts. There are instances where it may be appropriate to have separate accounts for certain things, such as child support. But this needs to be a joint decision satisfactory to both partners. One young wife told a friend that she kept a secret bank account in case she wanted to leave the marriage. It is pretty obvious that her marriage is in serious trouble.

Car Wars

The group gathered for our Newlywed seminar was shaken when Rob and Angela burst into the room with red faces and clenched fists. No doubt about it, they were in the middle of an extremely hot discussion. Angela was so upset over Rob's unexpected purchase of a new car that she was threatening divorce. Fortunately, they had agreed to come to the group and air their differences so there would be witnesses in case of murder!

Angela had assumed that they would discuss any large purchase. Rob was used to spending his own money without asking permission from anyone. That afternoon he had driven home in his new purchase, a red sports car. He had expected Angela to be thrilled. Instead, she was furious that he would make such a big decision without consulting her. She would certainly have had another type of car in mind.

We remained as quiet as possible until they had calmed down. As they talked, they began to see what had happened to them. Several of the couples related similar (but less drastic) situations they had experienced, and from this "real life drama," we were able to draw some helpful conclusions. Rob realized that he was no longer the Lone Ranger; he had to consider Angela's feelings. They both decided that they would no longer postpone their discussion on finances and priorities. They were ready to realistically come to an agreement on their goals, needs, and wants. I'm happy to report that Rob and Angela are still married and seem to have resolved their problems through improved communication.

Establishing a Budget

Now let's examine your financial goals. We have established that it is absolutely necessary to have a budget. Write down all regular, monthly expenses that you have and categorize them. Remember that this will not be "sealed in blood"; there will be changes along the way. Next, the two of you should prioritize your list and note what should be paid at the beginning and the middle of the month. Decide on fundamental rules for paying the bills. Be sure that you set aside some money for an emergency fund.

You will also need to make preparation for major purchases such as furniture or a car. This is where it is important to have your priorities as a couple down in writing. This will require flexibility and negotiating for both of you.

Of course, there will be a time when it will be necessary to borrow money. Not many people can buy a house, for example, without doing so. Be sure that you agree on the purchase and on the wisdom of the decision as well as on your ability to pay the price.

How can you learn to live on less? Here are some suggestions from those of us who have had to learn these lessons:

1. Learn to keep records. Invest in some manila folders, and develop a filing system that you both understand. This will help in preparing your income tax statement.
2. Resist shopping temptations (credit cards, 800 numbers, TV ads, etc.).
3. Food bills can be monitored. Many "instant, frozen, prepared" foods add greatly to the food budget. Learn to cook some basic nutritious meals. Don't go grocery shopping when hungry. Cut out as many "empty calorie" foods as possible.
4. Watch for big expenses. Try to plan ahead and be in agreement on these things to avoid conflict and resentment.
5. Do you have some hidden luxuries? These can take the form of pets and hobbies. Be sure you can afford these things.
6. What are your luxuries? Name yours. How much do they cost you? Are they worth it?

For You to Do

Respond to these statements and questions and then share your responses with your fiancé(e):

1. I can live on a budget. (yes, no)
2. I am a compulsive buyer. (yes, no)
3. I am a bargain hunter. (yes, no)
4. I am a big spender. (yes, no)
5. I am willing to take a risk. (yes, no)
6. I am "tight" with my money. (yes, no)
7. I am satisfied with my career/profession. (yes, no)

8. I will probably want to go back to school. (yes, no)
9. I am now living on a budget with success. (yes, no)
10. I am used to having my parents help with my expenses. (yes, no)
11. What is your total debt now? On a separate sheet of paper list your debts as follows: credit cards, tuition, housing, automobile, investments, hobbies, business, and any others that you may have.
12. How much money will it take for you to live as a couple (per month)?

There are many good books on the market to guide you in setting up your household budget. Find one that suits your needs. It will be a worthwhile purchase.

13

Talk to Me About: How We Communicate

Communication is the means by which we relate to one another. Good communicators have the ability to transmit and receive meanings. Have you ever been around a couple who seemed to have nothing in common? Perhaps they had at one time been compatible, but over a period of time they had grown apart, merely sharing the same house. What happened to them? Somewhere along the way, they stopped communicating with each other. We're talking about more than commenting on the weather or the laundry or the problems with the children. A couple can discuss those things while the deep feelings that need to be shared with a spouse are neglected.

Communication Gaps

In one of our groups, several of the men confessed that they found it hard to be open in discussing personal matters with their fiancées; they were accustomed to keeping everything to themselves. These men were in their mid-thirties and were finding it hard to trust the new special person in their lives.

Mary explained that when she is upset, she rants and raves and "lets it all hang out." Jim, on the other hand, keeps everything bottled up. Mary feels betrayed because she doesn't know what is going on in his mind.

A pastor friend of ours tells this story on himself. When he was in the seminary during the first year of marriage, his bride told him one morning, "I think we'll have beans for supper tonight." All day Ken thought about a simmering pot of Boston baked beans, anticipating the taste of his childhood. As he returned home, turned the key in the latch, and took one sniff, he knew that something was wrong. He sat down to green pole beans with bacon, cooked to death the Southern way. What a disappointment!

Fortunately, he and his wife were able to laugh at their miscommunication. However, if he had not told his bride what he thought she meant, she never would have known that he would like his kind of beans occasionally. She was happy to learn to bake beans the Boston way once she knew!

There are many opportunities for miscommunication. If you never tell your partner what you like, you can expect to harbor angry feelings and your spouse will never know what is wrong. Learn to talk and listen, listen and talk!

Communication Styles

It is important to set up good communication skills while you are still engaged. It is said that newlyweds fight about the way they talk—or don't talk—more than they fight about sex, friends, religion, job obligations, time together, or values. Communicating well is vital to a satisfying marital relationship. The way you communicate usually reflects your personality and your family's communication system. If you're outgoing, you may end up making most of the decisions simply because your style is more aggressive. If you are shy about expressing yourself, you may end up feeling used and depressed. If you both are outspoken and feel the need to have the last word, you may be constantly embroiled in battles.

The way you communicate can aggravate and confuse problems that you already have. Each person needs to understand that the other cannot be expected to know what he/she is thinking if it is not spoken clearly and heard accurately. It is not just the issue at hand, but how you deal with it. Do you attack each other? Do you clam up and avoid talking about it?

Do you "go along" and then get furious with yourself and your fiancé(e)?

Communicating well does not ensure a peaceful, conflict-free marriage. There is nothing unhealthy about disagreement. If there are two healthy, thinking individuals involved, there are bound to be disagreements. It is how you handle them that matters. It would be a very boring relationship if one partner or the other did all the thinking and decision making. The other partner would be just a blob! We want you to learn creative ways of communicating that will enhance your relationship and increase your admiration for each other. If you are not totally wrapped up in insisting that you know best, you may realize that you have a very smart and interesting partner. That's probably what attracted you to each other in the first place. Always try to find better ways to connect with each other, to feel closer, to become more understanding and better understood.

Two Problems

As we mentioned earlier, there are two basic types of problem communicators. One is overexpressive, the other is underexpressive. One is as bad as the other, and the goal for each should be to learn to truly listen to each other. Sometimes it is harder for the quiet one to learn to express himself than for the loud one to calm down! What matters is not how you act toward each other, but how you react. If you don't learn to react properly, you will end up attacking each other. If you are an expressive, "let it all hang out" couple, be sure that your open sharing of feelings is done with sensitivity and kindness rather than with attacks and taunts. Don't hurt each other with cutting words.

You may find that your fights get into strange communication cycles that lead nowhere except destruction. You will need to make a special effort to break these cycles. It takes a lot of control and a real desire to communicate without getting into situations that hurt one or both of you. Remember that you may be able to win an argument but you may lose your partner!

Here are some suggestions for learning to communicate in a healthy way. Remember that timing is important!

1. Don't mask the truth. "White lies" distort the issue
2. Look for the target of your anger; don't blame your anger on your partner. For example, you may be upset about moving but express anger about placement of furniture.
3. Tell your partner when you are upset. Say, "This upsets me. We need to talk about it." Don't expect another person to read your mind or automatically know when you are upset.
4. Take time to talk and listen to each other. Set aside time to be alone together. There are always new things to learn and ideas and dreams to share.
5. Say what is on your mind in a way that can be understood by your partner. He/she shouldn't have to decode any hidden messages.
6. Reflect your partner's feelings back to him/her so that she/he will feel understood. ("You must have had an awful day.")
7. Encourage your partner by being positive and understanding. We get enough negatives in the "outside world"; we need to feel loved and appreciated at home.
8. There will be times when you don't agree with each other. The goal of true communication is not necessarily total agreement. The goal should be to understand each other.
9. Try not to answer questions with a "yes" or "no." Ask non-threatening questions and try to give nonaccusatory answers.
10. There are times when it is best to let off steam before any serious communication takes place. If you are extremely tired or have had a hard day at the office, don't take it out on your spouse. He/she does not need to be your dumping ground. Go for a jog or a walk; have a cup of tea and read for a little while before you ruin a perfectly lovely evening!

For You to Do

1. Describe the communication in your parents' home. Do you think that it was satisfactory to your mother? To your father?

   a. Did they discuss issues loudly or quietly?
   b. Do you remember being upset or disturbed by their discussions?
   c. Did you learn good communication skills from them?

   Share your reactions with your fiancé(e).

2. Do you feel that you are able to communicate with each other now without feeling threatened or hurt?
3. Decide which of these statements apply to you and share with each other.

    a. I am too withdrawn.
    b. My fiancé(e) is too withdrawn.
    c. I am very emotional.
    d. My fiancé(e) is very emotional.
    e. I am a (good listener, not a good listener).
    f. My fiancé(e) is a (good listener, not a good listener)
    g. I handle conflicts by:
       ____ suffering in silence
       ____ screaming and throwing things
       ____ discussing things calmly
    h. My fiancé(e) handles conflict by:
       ____ suffering in silence
       ____ screaming and throwing things
       ____ discussing things calmly
    i. I tend to harbor grudges.
    j. My fiancé(e) tends to harbor grudges.

4. I will pledge to do my best to learn good communication skills. I realize that this requires practice, patience, and time. I truly want to understand my mate on a deeper level.

14

Talk to Me About: How You Handle Anger

The first step to good communication is the ability to control one's temper, to express anger and frustration appropriately. Many people have great difficulty in this area. We like to think that "nice people from nice homes" never resort to violence and always manage to keep their feelings under control. This is a myth that must be exposed. Help must be offered to those who are controlled by extreme anger. It is impossible to communicate with a person who is throwing things, screaming, or threatening the safety of others. Yes, there is communication going on, but it only generates fear, pain, and disgust. The dynamics operating among abusive courting couples are also shared by many married couples. On the other extreme, there are some very pious people who state that "Christian families never argue, fuss, or otherwise express anger." What boring families they must be! Couples who marry usually have many ideas and opinions in common, but it is natural that there will be times when you differ enough to argue.

Mishandled Anger

Anger is a normal part of life and nothing to be ashamed of. The way you handle anger is the all-important issue. Anger and hostility are the causes or the results of poor communication.

Anger, when kept under cover, will finally explode. This can occur in many different ways (sexual problems, psychosomatic illnesses, depression, an affair, "cutting each other down" in public, etc.).

Some couples seem to be constantly battling. It becomes difficult to determine the cause of the hostility. Sometimes it may be that one or the other desperately desires intimacy but is constantly sabotaging the opportunities. It is important for such couples to find the source of the hostility and take steps to improve the relationship.

Intimate Enemies

As I was standing at the checkout counter at the supermarket the other day, I witnessed an interesting scene. At the next counter a middle-aged couple was exchanging killer looks and blistering words. The minute they were confronted by the cashier and bag boy, they were pleasant and halted their battle. But as they carried their groceries to their car, they were at each other's throats again. We are all guilty of this sort of thing to some degree. Too often we are nicer to strangers than we are to our own family.

Eddie told me about his frustration with Betty. They had been married six months and even though Betty had been a very warm, loving person during the first six weeks of marriage, she was now distant and unresponsive. He couldn't figure out what went wrong. When he tried to be warm and loving, she would retreat.

Then Betty told me that married life was just not what she expected. She discovered that Eddie was only human after all, with a lot of frailties that she wasn't prepared for. She thought the fault must be hers, but she was angry that marriage was not what she had expected. She had not been able to admit this to Eddie, so she got more and more resentful each time he tried to be romantic.

After we were able to get Betty and Eddie to talk honestly about their feelings, they began to work on the situation and Betty was able to express what she felt. She found out that

Eddie was feeling the same disappointment. They are working on making their expectations for the relationship more realistic.

We fear anger because we are taught that it is wrong and we are afraid of losing control. We are afraid of the wrath of God. We can handle the fact of God's anger because we trust Him, knowing that He is just and fair and not vindictive. We should try to imitate God and behave in a trustworthy way when expressing anger.

Guidelines for Anger

Here are ways to express anger constructively:

- Be willing to truly listen as well as to talk.
- Stick to the subject at hand. Don't rake up old problems or deliberately try to wound each other.
- Never threaten to leave, go home to Mother, divorce, or commit suicide.
- Never resort to physical violence.
- Use tears sparingly. Tears can be a form of manipulation.
- If emotions threaten to get out of control, call a truce.
- Decide on an appropriate time to come back to the bargaining table.
- Sometimes one gives in to the wishes of the other. This is acceptable if it does not become the only way of resolving differences.
- Compromise (with good grace) is healthy if it motivates concessions in the future from both parties.
- You may never totally agree on some things. You may have to agree to disagree and work on a viable alternative. There will usually be one to whom the outcome is less important

Abusive Relationships

One of the hidden problems in families today is the presence of spouse or child abuse. Studies on premarital violence among couples on college campuses showed that sixty percent had either been a victim or a perpetrator of abuse in a dating relationship. The idea that "he wouldn't hit me if he didn't love me" seems to be operating among abusive college couples. There are some dynamics common to abusive couples; whether married or engaged:

a. A background of abusive behavior fostered in childhood (either having been abused, or observing abusive behavior).
b. An abnormal intensity in the relationship.
c. An implied right to influence one another.
d. A sense of male dominance over the female mind and body.
e. An extensive knowledge of the other person's frailties (both physical and emotional) and the use of these for purposes of attack.
f. Use of alcohol or drugs.
g. Frustrations experienced at work or elsewhere.
h. Cultural pressures for men to succeed and to be good providers.
i. Mental illness which has poor prognosis for correction.

There are cases of the abused husband. However, only three percent of husbands seeking a divorce cite physical abuse by their wives as a reason. Most abused husbands are ill, old, or smaller than the wife. Most often the husband is battered verbally and psychologically rather than physically. Many women caught in unfulfilling marriages resort to verbal battering in protest. Words do cause great pain and can provoke physical battering in return.

If you find yourself in an abusive relationship, you need to face the facts. No matter how hard you try, you will not be able to change your partner's abusive ways. He/she may promise to change, but it cannot be done without professional help. The remedy may be fairly simple, such as learning appropriate ways to handle anger and anticipate problem areas. You will have to work together on this, so you will need to see a counselor separately and together.

But the problem may not be so easily remedied. If the abusive person has been this way all of his/her life, or lived in an abusive situation, the problem may be very difficult to treat. You will have to decide how much you (and possibly your children) should endure. Remember that the longer you endure this situation, the sicker you yourself become. A person who continues to be the recipient of physical abuse needs to run, not walk, to seek professional counseling to understand why he/she tolerates it.

In a second marriage with a blended family, an abusive stepparent can cause grave damage. I know of one situation where the stepmother pinched her husband's little boys and caused terrible bruises (under the pants) when they visited on weekends. The father could not understand why his children cried when he went to pick them up. He found it hard to believe that his present wife was abusing them.

Your children may become the focus of your present spouse's anger and endure verbal, if not physical, abuse. Almost every week there are reports of a stepfather sexually abusing a girl. If a mother knows this and chooses to ignore it, she is also guilty of a terrible crime. Many times children have no choice but to bear the pain of abuse. The parent is responsible for the well-being of the child. This is also true when the child's other natural parent is the abuser.

Writer Lewis Grizzard quoted a letter he received from an inmate in the Georgia Women's Correctional Institute. This woman was the victim of physical abuse for years, having been literally tortured. She had finally shot her husband and was now in prison. This is her advice: "My message is, seek help. If you are a woman, talk to your family doctor, a minister, a psychologist, or a police officer. If you are a child and your mother is being abused, talk to your school counselor or minister or police. And just leave! Get away before it's too late."

You may be offended that we have dealt with abusive behavior at such length. However, there is overwhelming evidence that this type of behavior exists hidden in well-to-do and well-educated families as well as in poor and uneducated families. If it is not addressed and treated, it can go on for generations. The most appropriate time to deal with it is before marriage.

For You to Do

1. Tell each other how anger was handled in your parents' home.
2. How do you handle anger and frustration?
3. Do you feel that you need help in this area?
   Do you feel that your fiancé(e) needs help?
4. What are some things that trigger your anger?
5. Is it necessary for you to win an argument? If so, why (ego, self-esteem, etc.)?
6. Separately write down some ground rules for settling arguments. Compare and combine where appropriate.

15

Nurturing Intimacy

Intimacy is a rare commodity. Intimacy is usually desired more than wealth and it certainly cannot be bought. A relationship of growing intimacy develops when two people are determined to work at the relationship and turn their "separateness" into a bond of close communion.

Family Patterns

There are many experiences in life that will affect one's ability to allow intimacy. These experiences influence the way you visualize your ideal intimate relationship. The first to consider is how you were treated as a child by close family members. If you experienced feelings of abandonment, you may need desperately to feel the security of trusting and depending on someone. If love was expressed through confrontation and fighting in your childhood family, you may seek intimacy in the same way. When two people have differing childhood experiences, it may require time and a lot of communication to understand the needs of each other.

John was distressed by what he saw developing in his marriage to Cindy. He had difficulty persuading her to sit in front of the fire to talk over the things that were important to him. He wanted to dream about their future. He wanted to learn about Cindy.

Cindy saw this as John's attempt to control her, and she

could not respond as he wished. The only time she was able to say anything important was in the heat of an argument. John learned more about her during fights than was ever possible in normal communication. After a fight, Cindy was always warm and mellow and enjoyed making love. In bed, after a heated argument that was followed by passionate love, was Cindy's time to open up and be responsive.

Cindy agreed to talk to a marriage counselor about the situation. She learned that the reason she responded to John's desire for intimacy as she did had its roots in her childhood. She had seen her mother and father engage in terrible arguments that would finally end in an emotional reconciliation. It was the only time she was aware that her parents expressed any concern for each other. After John understood what was going on and Cindy was willing to change, they worked on ways to change their patterns and learned to relate intimately in ways that were more acceptable to both of them.

There are different attitudes about what intimacy is and how it is attained among men and women. Generally speaking, men are threatened by intimacy while women are threatened by separation. Women want more of a sharing relationship with their mates; they need a feeling of being connected in order to feel loved. Men spend time talking and listening before marriage in the way that fosters the growth of intimacy, but they are often unwilling to spend time after marriage on communicating in the same way.

Past Relationships

Another experience that influences the way you relate is whether you have been disappointed in past relationships. If you have been married before or have had a long-term relationship, try to reconstruct your relational patterns and determine what didn't work for you.

Your personality type will be a significant element in your ability to relate to others in a healthy way. Some people are "overexpressive" and some are "underexpressive." Some need constant attention and emotional reinforcement and others are passive and withdrawn. Each type can adjust and learn to express true, loving feelings without overwhelming or "under-whelming" the other.

Life Stages

Depth of intimacy is also determined by your stage of life. Loss of a job, loss of a parent, pregnancy, career change, a friend's terminal illness are all life cycle situations that affect one's intimacy needs.

One couple who came to our Newlywed seminar had a sad experience. They had been married about six weeks when they joined the group. They came for several weeks and then missed two or three times. They sent word that the husband's mother had died and that he was tied up with his family. Then we received a call from the wife, in tears, saying that he had told her that he just couldn't handle being married while dealing with his mother's death. She had made every effort to be supportive and told him that she would wait for him to overcome his grief so that they could start over. He finally insisted on a divorce after refusing to go for counseling. An unusual but actual situation, it shows that people react in strange ways to grief.

Several years ago, a pastor friend and his wife suddenly got a divorce. Everyone was shocked. Their second child, a son, had just died after a long battle with cancer. There was a compound tragedy—the loss of a child and the loss of a spouse. This couple's relationship had been so bound up in the care of the child that they had nothing left for the marriage. It seems that they focused the anger they felt over their son's illness and death on each other. It has been a sad situation for both of them. And a surviving child has had severe emotional problems stemming from the death and divorce.

If you ever experience the serious illness or death of a loved one, be sure to seek counseling so that displaced anger and unresolved grief will not harm your marriage. Sometimes the very things that should increase intimacy prove to be too painful to share. In order to ease the pain, one may try to forget by withdrawing from a mate or leaving altogether.

The same problems exist when there has been a career

reversal. The loss of a job increases dependency on each other in ways that the couple may not be equipped to handle. One critical situation very often creates another. Our emotions are raw, and it is difficult and embarrassing to admit anger, defeat, and fear to those we love the most.

Trying times like these can be turned into opportunities for deeper communication that will draw you closer together. As you get older and live together longer, you will become more creative in finding ways to express your love and support for one another. This is one of the things that make marriage such an exciting adventure.

Connected or Separate

Individuals who have been single for a number of years may find the prospect of marital intimacy threatening. Couples make countless decisions that determine whether they will function as a unit or remain two separate individuals. Day-to-day questions such as: Should we always visit relatives together; will the wife change her name; will we do everything together; how will we use our vacation time, will determine the degree of mutual dependence. The key to success is to find the right balance between separateness and connectedness. Just being together during routine activities can be very special if the time is shared in a loving, supportive way.

It is important to talk to each other, listen to each other, and share your innermost feelings. Of course, you will never divulge these private secrets to anyone else, including parents or friends. This would break the trust relationship so vital for true intimacy. You become a special unit when you have shared your heart's desires and your most private dreams with each other.

There will be times when the two of you won't be on the same wavelength because of career pressures, family responsibilities, or any number of things. Try to be understanding and allow each other to have space when needed. However, this should not go on for an extended period of time; the longer it continues, the harder it will be to regain the unit feeling. Always remember that you are both individuals with your own ideas, your own "'sense of self" that makes the union interesting. Differing opinions and experiences add to the strength of the union and can create a greater desire for intimacy.

Deepening Intimacy

From the groups of newlyweds we have counseled, we have gathered some suggestions for deepening intimacy. You will be able to add some of your own.

- Choose to sit close to each other in a restaurant rather than across the table.
- Leave a note where it will be found.
- Prepare a favorite dish; remember to carry out the trash.
- Try a tender touch, a fond glance, a nod or wink across the room.
- Bring a surprise occasionally. It doesn't have to be expensive to say you care.
- Make private time for each other. Plan special events.
- Begin now to share each other's interests as well as develop some new common interests.
- Find ways to reassure your spouse that you are trustworthy.

For You to Do

Individual need for intimacy varies greatly from person to person. It will be helpful to clarify your intimacy expectations with each other. Think about these questions individually and then discuss them together.

1. Should you spend *all* of your free time together?
2. Should you *always* visit relatives together, or will it be all right if each sometimes goes alone?
3. Do you feel comfortable sharing your innermost thoughts with your fiancé(e)? Do you feel that you can trust him/her not to tell anyone else?
4. What "baggage" are you bringing with you into the marriage that may affect your attitude toward intimacy? For example:

   a. Did you grow up in a very protected environment?
   b. Will you expect to be nurtured in the same way?
   c. Are you a very independent person who enjoys a lot of "space"?

    d. Do you want to have input in all financial decisions because your family is marginal financially?

    e. Are you very close to your parents/family and will you have a hard time separating yourself from your present place in the family circle?

5. How are you nurturing and building intimacy in your relationship? List some specific ways you will increase intimacy after you are married.

16

Talk to Me About: Sex

This chapter is not intended to be a chapter on sexual techniques. There are more than enough helpful books on that topic. The main thing we'd like you to learn from this chapter is this: You have permission to enjoy sex with your spouse. In fact, we *encourage* you to have fun, to delight in each other sexually.

Some people seem to approach married sex with great seriousness. It is something to be endured or it should be evaluated according to the latest magazine article on sexual fulfillment. We say: Relax, have fun, communicate your needs and desires to each other, and you'll experience sexual satisfaction.

Private Joy

One of the greatest things about sex is the feeling of warmth, intimacy, the joy of really knowing your loved one in the most intimate way possible. It is your secret life together. It is special in that you know each other in ways that no one else can ever know you. It binds you together and yet releases you to be a better "you."

Life has a way of making us very serious. It's serious business to keep on top of your career, keep your social life going, maintain a home, buy groceries and cook meals, care for children, *and* make time for each other. The world makes sure that we remember that life is serious. Someone at work will make it their job to keep you humble, the furnace will break down on the weekend in the dead of winter, the baby will cry all night, and your mother will call to remind you of your duty to your parents. Need I go on?

So the time you have together should be fun. Nobody else is going to see to it that you have any fun or pleasure. Sex in marriage is God's gift to allow you to experience the sheer joy of intimately loving and caring for your spouse. It can be exciting and thrilling or it can be as dull as the rest of your life. It's up to the two of you to be free to do whatever delights, pleases, and satisfies *each other*. There is liberty in marriage for both the man and woman to experience all of the joyful aspects of sex.

Successful Sex

There has to be *sexual attraction* that makes you want to get married. You don't want someone just to be your roommate or housekeeper or breadwinner. You are attracted to this person both physically and spiritually. This may come about immediately or may grow from friendship. A college friend of mine got involved with a young man on campus who was just a pitiful person. He looked as if he had been standing in the rain with no protection. He had a bedraggled personality as well, and sort of whined when he talked. Doris took him as her project. She finally married him because she felt that he couldn't stand it if she deserted him. The relationship appears to be one where she takes care of him. She provides the income and he feels poorly most of the time. She could have done the same thing for a brother or parent and had a better life. So don't be hooked on the "he/she needs me to take care of him/her" argument. There has to be that passion or there will be no sparks and fun.

The glamorous, falling-in-love, passionate sex that should be present in marriage can quickly fade into routine sex with overtones of duty. Certainly life has to be more than a continuous romp in bed, but couples need to pledge to each other that, as a reward for getting through the "dailyness" of life, they will continually explore and enjoy the recreation and intimacy of sex. The time of relaxed intimacy brings the added pleasure of feeling each other's vulnerability. This is a safe, secure time, a good time for sharing one's innermost thoughts and dreams. Shared dreams make all aspects of marriage more pleasurable.

None of the above can come about unless each partner is absolutely and *unalterably monogamous*. If you love your partner deeply and have pledged your committed love to him/her, there must never be even a hint that you would do anything to risk losing the trust and respect of your loved one. True love must be based on trust, faith, and fidelity.

There are some people who seem to believe that they are driven by hormones. They act as if they shouldn't be expected to limit their sexual appetites in any way. That is just an excuse for their refusal to make a life commitment to another person. Some feel that they should have the option to play around after marriage. These are the immature ones whose lives are usually a mess. Trouble in the sexual area, difficulty in being committed to one person, usually reflects problems in other areas.

Once you have vowed to be faithful, true, monogamous, then that decision is made and you should never have to make it again. When you are attracted to another person or tempted to be unfaithful to your spouse, you should not have to stop and think. The decision has been made and there is no question about it: You *will* be faithful and true. You are secure in that knowledge and so is your spouse. Think of all the lies you won't have to tell! Think of how special and sacred your marriage is to you both. It is not difficult to be faithful once the decision is made. A marriage built on less than fidelity will not be worth having.

Previous Sexual Experience

Couples come to the marriage altar today with all degrees of sexual experience. In the "olden days" it was assumed (but not necessarily true) that at least the bride was a virgin. Today it is well known that a lot of couples live together before marriage, some of them in serial relationships.

Living together is not the best preparation for marriage. The latest secular articles and books verify the fact that couples who live together before marriage are more likely to divorce than those who do not. One survey showed that the longer a woman lived with her partner before marriage, the more prone the marriage to end in divorce.

There is a lot of difference in a relationship before and after marriage. Marriage signifies to the world that this is a legitimate relationship, one that should endure until "death do us part." The relationship changes from independence to greater dependence on each other, and rising expectations. This can create friction and a sense of being "hemmed in" by the other partner. Couples who have lived together may need special counseling to make the adjustment.

There are still both men and women who come to marriage as virgins. There may be problems at first with both being nervous and unskilled, but in the long run, these couples have the advantage of learning together, of knowing that they are not being compared with anyone else. They have the joy of sharing the thrill of the unknown, of making discoveries together.

Whatever your situation, decide now that you will be faithful to each other. It is dangerous psychologically and physically to do otherwise.

The AIDS Factor

Joe was a young single man on this way up in the corporate world. He was a dear person, sensitive and caring, but he also enjoyed playing the field with girlfriends. He considered himself God's gift to women. His job required that he travel a lot, and he developed relationships in a number of cities around the country. Not long ago, we attended Joe's funeral. He died of AIDS, contracted from one of his girlfriends who also had multiple relationships. We wonder if his other girlfriends know he had AIDS . . . and what about their current boyfriends?

This also happens to married couples. A business trip fling can turn into a nightmare. One of our clients came to us in total devastation. Her doctor had just verified that she has herpes, for which there is no known cure. The contact had to be sexual, and it turned out that her husband admitted to a "one night stand" on a business trip. The fact is that when you have sex with someone, you are also having sex with everyone they have slept with.

Phil made an appointment with his pastor and sat weeping in his office. He was scared to death that he had AIDS. He had had every test possible and there was some delay in the results. He had a history of visiting high-priced call girls and was afraid that the disease had caught up with him. Not only was he fearful for his health, but should he tell his wife?

The results of indiscretions are not worth the price that has to be paid in health problems, mental and emotional anguish, and damaged relationships.

Unwanted Pregnancies

Linda sat in her doctor's office not believing what he had just confirmed. She was pregnant. She was separated from her husband and had been having an affair with one of the men in her office. When she had told him that she might be pregnant, he told her that she was on her own. He was a married man and had no intention of getting a divorce to marry her. Linda was faced with a humiliating situation. Her doctor didn't see her again for almost a year. She had left his office for an abortion clinic. Now she needed help for chronic infections.

In another situation, I sat holding an adorable little girl. My friend had been wanting a baby for so long and here she was . . . an adopted baby. The teenage mother had decided to give this precious baby to parents who could give her love and security. The girl knew she wasn't ready to marry a teenage boyfriend and add to her mistakes. This baby was a mistake for the young girl, but a blessing to this young couple.

One of the serious areas of concern for young couples is the matter of birth control. With so much information available these days, we assume that everyone knows everything. That really isn't true. Be sure that both of you have a physical examination before marriage and ask for advice on birth control. This cannot be put off until later. When you have agreed on an acceptable method, be open to change if it doesn't prove satisfactory to both. If it leaves you feeling nervous about an unwanted pregnancy or interferes too much with spontaneous sex, then perhaps there is a better solution.

Homosexuality

There is another problem that should be avoided in marriage. Numerous marriages end in divorce because one spouse becomes involved in a same-sex affair. This is probably even more devastating to a marriage relationship than a heterosexual affair. We have counseled with couples planning to marry when we sensed that there might be a sexual identity problem. When this is addressed, it may be denied. If acknowledged, the couple may insist that a good marriage will change the situation. It never does. It will bring nothing but heartache and problems. If there is any suspicion of a sexual identity problem with either partner, seek professional counseling before there is a wedding. There can be no true integrating of souls in marriage unless both are exclusively heterosexual.

Ernie and Babs seemed to be a normal couple with two cute little boys. They both were active in church and civic organizations. It was a shock to all who knew them when Babs suddenly left home to live with another woman. When Ernie came for counseling, he said that he had early accepted the fact that Babs had no desire for sex with him. The straw that broke his back was when she demanded that he allow her female friend to move in with her and he move to another bedroom. They could all live together! After a number of years Ernie remarried and has a beautiful relationship, which he certainly deserves. The children have been in therapy for years to deal with this situation.

If you are unsure of your sexuality, seek counseling and become a whole person before attempting marriage.

Sexuality and Spirituality

The Bible has a lot to say about sexuality. It goes hand in hand with spirituality. From the creation story in Genesis right through the New Testament, we see that the Bible celebrates human sexuality. First we are told that we are special, created in the image of God! Our sexuality, male and female, is related to God through the creation. "For this reason a man will leave his father and mother and be united to his wife, and they will become one flesh. The man and his wife were both naked, and they felt no shame." (Genesis 2:24, 25 NIV). The man and woman were drawn to one another, were naked and not ashamed. We were created to love.

The Song of Solomon is a sensual, passionate celebration of erotic love. This beautiful love story describes the longing for one's lover, the beauty of bringing chastity to the marriage, the satisfaction in the passion of both partners, and the fact that love is permanent: "a seal over your heart . . . love is as strong as death . . ." (Song of Solomon 8:6).

The sanctity of marriage and the relationship of husband and wife are held in the highest regard in the New Testament as we see from the teachings of Jesus. Jesus added to the creation story by saying, "So they are no longer two, but one [flesh]. Therefore, what God has joined together, let man not separate" (Matthew 19:6 NIV). In Hebrews is this statement: "Let marriage be held in honor among all, and let the marriage bed be undefiled; for God will judge the immoral and adulterous" (Hebrews 13:4 RSV).

Claim the Gift!

Sex in marriage . . . the gift of God . . . ours to claim. Relax, be flexible, take time, and have fun! In order to claim this gift there are some things to remember:

- Find time for sex. Life gets so hectic and important responsibilities can fill both days and nights to the brim. You really can be "too tired" for sex. Remember that you manage to make time for other important things. This is important, too, and could prove to be crucial to the happiness of your marriage. You may have to learn to say "no" to family and friends and "yes" to your lover!
- Make your surroundings conducive to spontaneous sex. Don't swathe yourself in layers of pajamas and gowns . . . be available. Touching and snuggling are enjoyable and comforting and may lead

to something interesting! Clean sheets and clean, nice-smelling bodies go well together.

- If you have children, get a sitter and go out on a date. Talk about things other than the children or household details. Do something romantic. Take a walk, hold hands at the movies, tell each other something special that you admire in each other, be attentive as you were when you were dating.
- Remember that lovemaking is tied to all parts of life. Tension in this area may be a sign that there are problems somewhere else. If you are angry, you can't be as open and warm. Tell your spouse what is bothering you and work it out.
- Resolve to be open and honest with each other in talking about sex. Trust your partner to care enough to listen and you do the same.
- Sexuality is closely related to how we see ourselves. Too many times a man or woman has said, "It really doesn't matter how I look now that we are married. He/she has to love me just the way I am." Desire for sex diminishes when one or the other becomes excessively fat or lets their grooming become sloppy. Looking good and being well groomed not only speaks loudly about how you feel about yourself but also how you feel about your spouse.

For You to Do

Respond to the following statements and discuss your responses with your fiancé(e):

1. I believe in an unalterably monogamous relationship.
2. My parents were open and loving with each other . . . or
   My parents never exhibited any feeling for each other.
3. I am ready to be faithful to my fiancé(e).
4. We will each have a physical examination and agree on an acceptable method of birth control.
5. Our marriage ceremony will signify the fact that I plan to make love to the same person for the rest of my life.
6. I will covenant that I will do my part in making sex a wonderful, creative expression of our committed love.

17

Talk to Me About: Our Relationship—Traditional or Partnership?

There is an inside joke in our family that takes place at the dinner table. One of the men (my husband or one of our two sons) will shake the ice in his empty tea glass and wait to see who will volunteer to get up for a refill. This began when a lovely young woman lived with us one summer when the boys were home from college. Quite by accident, one of them idly shook his empty tea glass and the ice rattled. Before any of us knew what happened, Gale got up and refilled his glass. He looked at her with amazement and before long this rattling of the ice was repeated by the other son, with the same result. We were all consumed with curiosity about this reflex action in Gale. She laughingly told us (but it was serious) that she grew up as the only girl in a rather large family of boys, including father and uncles. As the "girl baby," it was her duty to see to the needs of the men at the table. Thus, they would rattle the ice in their glasses as a signal for her to get more tea! That's what "girl babies" were for in that family! The male/female roles may not be that obvious in your family, but every family has them and you will discover them in your own reactions.

Traditional Roles

There was a time not too many years ago when the marriage ceremony signaled the assumption of the traditional American male/female roles. Traditionally, the hardworking husband was supposed to come home to find dinner waiting on the table, in a house that was tended by his domesticated wife. In America, we don't have a "wife school" as they do in some tribal countries, but through many generations of tradition-bound homes, we have maintained the belief (if not the fact) that the old ways are more desirable than all the new "liberated roles." Today many wives are working, and they probably would love to have their husbands cook dinner, shop for groceries, and share responsibility for some of the household chores. The rules about who does what around the house are no longer ironclad. Each couple must decide for themselves which jobs will be the husband's responsibility and which will be the wife's. Job assignments may change with changing circumstances. Flexibility is doubly important in this area.

Modern Ambivalence

Today's young couples reach maturity in an age when one set of ideals is espoused, but they grew up in a time when another set of ideals was valued. Both men and women feel ambivalent in today's society. There is a part of you that wants to be very modern and career-oriented and another part that wants to be very tradition-bound. Often, both male and female feel this way. If you are to be a dual-career couple, both of you will need to modify your ideas and feelings about male and female roles.

Actually, children are shaped by the attributes of both parents, not just the one of the same sex. Boys spend a lot of their early formative years with their mother, thereby gaining the emotional nurturing skills generally associated with the female. This, added to the aggressive, competitive traits usually exhibited by the father, can provide the necessary skills for a modern partnership marriage. Marriage for many is a relationship that confirms their sexual identity and broadens their view of gender identity roles.

Partnership Marriages

Couples who see their marriage relationship as a partnership offer each other the best of both male and female worlds. In mature marriages, each person is able to lean on the other, and in turn be leaned on when that is necessary. Interdependence promotes a balance of power in a marriage. Partnership is needed in the relationship to best nurture the personhood of both male and female. Each is the reflection of the love, respect, and acceptance of the other. Each should be willing to give and take in the relationship for the good of the marriage.

Dual-career couples are under great stress because of the pressures to succeed at work and maintain friendships, as well as to build a happy marital relationship. Too often both spouses suffer from a lack of time and energy, and the burden of household responsibilities can seem overwhelming. The two of you may have difficulty agreeing on how to solve these conflicts. These differences cannot be continually ignored, so plan now to face them without going to war. Now is the time to find out each other's ideas of what constitutes a smoothly run household and how you plan to achieve that.

Being flexible about sex roles reduces stress caused by role strain. It has been said that women who work at jobs that require decision making and who are high achievers usually have better health than those who have more "humdrum" jobs. A man will also benefit when he can help out at home and assist his wife's career. Being supportive of each other, plus the stimulation of significant jobs or careers, makes married life more enjoyable, and promotes the health of both!

The old, traditional sex roles give only a single outlet for a person's talents. The key to being successful as a dual-career couple is flexibility. There may be a time when one may feel the need to slow down the career and emphasize child rearing for a few years. This should have the support of both partners. Partnership marriages enable a couple to make changes in their roles and to encourage each other to be their best at every step of life.

Flexibility Required!

Jan and Bert were in their mid-thirties when they married. One of the most important discussions they had was whether or not to have children. Both had flourishing careers and Jan had never had any desire to experience motherhood. Since Bert was rather neutral about the issue, they had decided never to have children. Suddenly, after a year or so of marriage, Jan's perspective changed. She wanted to have a baby and time was running out! To her dismay, the doctor told her that she probably could not get pregnant. But miracles do happen, and Jan got pregnant and delivered a healthy baby boy. Sixteen months later, an adorable little girl was born.

Then Jan and Bert began the wrenching experience of searching for suitable day-care facilities. Jan finally decided that no one was better qualified to care for her children than she, so she put her career on the shelf and plunged into full-time motherhood. The children are now three and four and Jan is making plans to reinstate her career gradually.

Jan and Bert have been interesting to observe. They have undergone tremendous changes and seem to thrive on it. Career couples who have children face the situation many different ways, but none is ever prepared for the impact that having a baby will make on you!

Your marriage will be uniquely yours. It will not be like that of your parents or any of your friends. This is your opportunity to be truly creative. Have fun while growing in this exciting new venture.

For You to Do

1. What is your idea of a traditional marriage? Of a partnership marriage?
2. How do you envision your marital relationship?
3. Describe to each other the roles that your parents played in your home.
4. Talk to each other about how to handle household chores. Make a list of things that have to be done such as: buying groceries; preparing breakfast and dinner; cleaning the kitchen; cleaning the bathroom; etc. Who will do each of these?
5. As you think about household chores, check yourself on these points: (a) Are you obsessive about a clean house? (b) As the wife, would you try to be a successful career person and a perfect homemaker? (c) As the husband, would you expect your spouse to take charge of housekeeping?

18

Talk to Me About: Relationships With Family and Friends

A good mother-in-law or father-in-law is one who accepts the son-in-law or daughter-in-law as one of the family, leaves the couple free to make their own choices (even their own mistakes), and depends upon example as the best teacher for the young couple. Dr. Lofton Hudson, longtime marriage counselor, suggests that this is often very difficult for parents. When a parent has guided, supported, and loved for so many years, it is hard to relinquish the responsibility.

But the young couple must stand on their own. The wise parent is mature enough to stand by a couple while standing out of their way. Some parents have ways of subtly encouraging their married children to cling to them. Mature parents realize that they are not successful as parents until their children are functioning as mature adults.

The Parent Trap

If your mother and father have always been the type to intervene in your life, don't expect that attitude to stop when you get married. There are many ways that parents manage to retain control of your life. Sometimes it is very subtle, and it may be some time before you realize what is going on.

Here is an example: You need new bathroom accessories

(shower curtains, window curtains, etc.) and your mother is aware of this. One evening when you come home from work and go to the bathroom, there it is—all done—and it isn't what you had in mind at all. Or perhaps it is given as a gift for you to open and you ask if you can exchange it for a different color. Your mother is crushed because your taste has changed. She used to be able to choose things and you liked them!

Or perhaps you have decided to shop for a new dress and Mother offers to go along and maybe even buy it for you. Your choice does not meet her approval, but rather than face her hurt feelings you choose one to her liking. The interesting thing is that her mother (or mother-in-law) did the same thing to her and she hated it and vowed she would never be that way . . . but it has come full circle to you. Perhaps you will be the one to break the chain.

This applies to sons as well. The best solution is to be open and honest with your parents with the goal of learning how to relate to each other in an adult way. Parents forget how important it is for children to make their own choices, good or bad, to gain experience, and develop skills in decision making.

Family Loyalty

One potentially dangerous in-law situation is when the husband is the only son (or favorite) of a widow. Often the mother and son are very close, and the mother may feel left out of the new relationship. The son doesn't want to hurt his mother, but he may face a difficult situation with his wife. However, it is up to the new husband to act on the fact that his wife is now the most important person in his life.

I vividly remember our Sunday afternoons when I was a child. They never varied. After lunch we got in the car and drove a short distance to visit with my father's mother, who lived with his sister's family. We usually stayed for several hours before leaving to drive on about eight miles to see my mother's parents. By the time we arrived, my father was anxious to get home in time for evening church services. The atmosphere in the car was always strained and unhappy, but our Sunday schedule remained the same. Mandatory visits can take away the pleasure of family relationships. It is unfair for parents to insist on a weekly family gathering.

Vacationing with in-laws can be hard on the family relationship. Perhaps you should discuss how you can be with your family (if they live out of town) without using all your vacation time for this. Some ground rules should be set and discussed honestly before going away on a vacation trip with family. Such a trip can overwhelm the relationship.

A whole new realm of in-law problems will surface when the first grandchild arrives. It is almost impossible for grandparents to refrain from offering advice and to restrain themselves when your parenting differs from theirs. If you have established a good, honest relationship, this new situation can be resolved to the satisfaction of all concerned.

Engagement Encounters

Use your engagement period to get to know your future in-laws. Don't expect to see eye to eye on everything, but try to appreciate their positive qualities. After all, they did produce the one you love and plan to marry. Be as courteous, thoughtful, and helpful as you can be. Treat them with the same consideration and respect that you give your friends. When they give advice, try to respond as you would to a friend; if it is good advice, follow it and thank them. If it is not, thank them for their concern and do what you choose. We all have the right to accept or reject advice, even the advice that we seek.

The tone of the relationship among you, your spouse, and your respective parents is set now. A serious hurt could be a barrier that cannot be erased with a marriage ceremony. On the other hand, it is possible for the in-law relationship to be even more rewarding than your own family relationship.

Attitudes toward your own parents may need to be examined. Perhaps you need to make peace with them. Families are so wonderful when all the people are mature and secure and know how to be loving without being smothering. Couples who are able to have good relationships with their in-laws are strengthened. It is marvelous to have family with whom to share life's joys and sorrows.

"Mom and Dad"?

Something that should be discussed as the wedding ceremony approaches is the matter of how you will address your in-laws. Will you continue to call them Mr. and Mrs.? Do they expect you to call them Mom or Dad, and will you be able to do that without feeling disloyal to your own parents? What about using their given names? Is that more comfortable? The important thing is that you decide on something that will be acceptable to both you and your future in-laws. I find that more and more young couples are using their in-laws' given names. Our own two daughters-in-law address us as Bill and Carolyn, and it feels very comfortable to us. The disturbing situation is when you don't know what to call your parents-in-law and refer to them in the third person. Names are important, and they can help set the tone of your relationship.

All the parties involved are responsible for making the in-law relationship a healthy one. A happy in-law experience doesn't just happen. It takes skill, patience, determination, and grace on the part of all concerned.

Changing Friendships

Friends, like family, are also important both before and after marriage. In the longest and best marital relationships, the husband and wife consider each other their best friend. But that does not eliminate the need for other friends. Different people bring out different facets of our personalities and make us more interesting to be around.

As you approach marriage, the question of "your" friends and "my" friends can create some interesting problems. One may feel threatened by a friend who is being brought into the relationship. Marriage will be a turning point for many of your friendships.

You may not realize that friendships may change until well into the first year of marriage. Some adjustments will happen naturally. You'll discover that there won't be as much in common with your single friends, and it will be harder to find time to be with them. They may feel threatened by your marriage and cool the relationship. If you sense that a certain friendship is creating jealousy or resentment on the part of your spouse, be sure to talk about it and decide how this can be handled. Unless your spouse is being totally unreasonable, you must remember that your mate is the most important person in your life; others will have to fall into line behind that commitment. Arrange to be with friends with whom your spouse has nothing in common when it will not interfere with your time as a couple. Close friends, male or female, should not divulge intimate details of the marriage relationship. There are secrets in a marriage that should never be shared with anyone else.

Many times the wife turns some of her personal friendships into family friendships by arranging social events involving the spouses. If this works and is a happy experience for everyone, it provides long-term continuity of friendships. It is unusual but wonderful when both husband and wife enjoy a deep friendship with one spouse's childhood friend.

Bill and I have been blessed with a very special friendship. Anne and I grew up together and were sorority sisters and roommates in college. Bill also became friends with Anne in college and knew her family. Anne met and married a young man from south Georgia and has lived there since. We have always been like sisters and so as we have visited back and forth, the four of us have developed a very special relationship. We are so close that their son, living with us while attending graduate school in our city, declared that "living at the Self house was just like living at the King house." This kind of friendship enhances both the friendship and the marriage. It can't be forced . . . it just happens.

Young married couples should get involved in organizations that will enable them to make mutual friends. Our Newlywed church school department provides couples with the opportunity to meet other couples in similar situations. We see lifelong friendships formed here.

Pressure Points

Finding time to get together with old (or new) friends is difficult because everyone is so involved with the new marriage relationship, developing their careers, keeping up with family, and even attending school. It becomes a challenge to be creative in planning and scheduling social events. You'll soon discover that you'll see less of friends who are not close to you both.

Opposite-sex friendships that are maintained after marriage can sometimes be threatening to the other spouse. Platonic friendships certainly can exist, but if the relationship is strong, it may become sexual. If your opposite-sex friendship creates anger, jealousy, fear, and frustration in your spouse, talk reasonably about it and keep in mind that your spouse is your priority. You do not want to cause him/her pain. It takes caution and awareness to keep such friendships from becoming more than platonic.

Sue complained that when her husband had a night out with the boys, it meant a lot of drinking and gambling. He came home poorer and inebriated. She had grown to dislike his "good old boy" friends immensely. She became enraged when he planned an evening with them.

Jerry is determined not to go out with his wife's best friend and her husband anymore. He has absolutely nothing in common with him and finds the evening a complete waste. His wife is angry at him and accuses him of not trying to make conversation.

Debbie hates to go to parties because John always flirts with his old girlfriends. John insists that he just enjoys keeping up with old friends. He is not aware of how deeply he is hurting Debbie.

Nell married a man who is fifteen years her senior. He is still close friends with two couples who were close friends and traveling companions with him and his first wife. Nell does not feel accepted by these people. The women seem to view her as competition and act as if she is trying to seduce their husbands. The husbands are amused and a little jealous that their old friend landed such a pretty young woman. The women are sure that she married him for his money. Nell understandably is uncomfortable in their presence.

As you can see, friends can do a lot to help a marriage or they can cause problems and deep wounds. Confront this topic now before you marry. Determine to meet new couples and make new friends together.

For You to Do

Family

1. Individually, reflect on your relationship with your own parents. Are you dependent on them? Are they manipulative or controlling? How do you respond to this? How do you relate to your siblings? Are you considered a close-knit family? Will your spouse be accepted as a peer?
2. Think of some positive qualities of your future in-laws. Share these with each other.
3. If your parents are aging or live nearby, you will need to discuss how you will relate to them in light of their needs. Be willing to compromise.
4. What will be your response if your relatives talk about your spouse behind his/her back? Relatives may be jealous of your new relationship. Will you be able to make it clear that your spouse comes first?
5. How close a relationship do you want with your families? If you want it to be close, how can you encourage that? If you prefer to preserve your privacy, how can you encourage that? How can you establish privacy without damaging family ties?

Friends

1. List on paper the friends who are important to you.
2. How often do you see these friends? Realistically, do you think you will be able to see them as often after you marry?
3. Are you pleased with the way your fiancé(e)'s friends treat you?
4. Do you now have many mutual friends?
5. Are most of your friends married or single?
6. How important do you think friends are?
7. Talk about how you think friends will impact your relationship.

19

Talk to Me About: Religion

Some people find it difficult to talk about their religious faith to anyone, including a fiancé(e) or spouse. For this reason, a couple often find themselves in love and considering marriage before they know each other's spiritual commitments.

Up until about 1965, most Americans assumed it was important for married couples to have similar religious beliefs. "Mixed marriages" were frowned upon and expected to encounter great difficulty. Today, all too often a marriage ceremony is performed in church only to please parents and grandparents. It should not be assumed that just because the minister delivers the warning, "What God has joined together, let no one put asunder," God had much to do with the joining together. Most likely, He was never consulted.

Marriage: Ordained by God

American family life would be greatly strengthened if couples anticipating marriage understood that marriage is not a civil ceremony; it is a sacred, religious thing, ordained by God and regulated by the state. When a minister leads a couple in taking their vows, it is the church participating in the holiest of relationships.

The biblical warning against being "yoked together" (2 Corinthians 6:14) with an unbeliever is not only good spiritual advice but solid practical counsel as well. To a great extent, a person's ability to develop and nurture a personal relationship depends on his relationship with God. Intimacy on the horizontal level and intimacy on the vertical level reinforce and complement each other. When one trusts God, he can more easily trust his spouse. Shared religion is a strengthening agent in marriage. There are numerous studies which show a great correlation between church attendance and marital stability. Worship is nurturing and trust-restoring; it undergirds the values of the family.

The way a person responds to the pressures of life depends a great deal on his/her spiritual health. People who are not able to trust God are likely to fall apart when life becomes difficult. The ability to face crises depends on spiritual resources and religious maturity.

When a couple shares a spiritual commitment, they find a transforming power and understanding that brings total unity to the marriage relationship. It is true that spiritual awareness and religious commitment are a growing part of life. People change and mature as the years go by. New understanding and maturity will occur at different times in the life cycles of each person. But to enter a marriage relationship hoping your spouse will eventually change and "see it your way" is to start on a very shaky foundation. On the other hand, you may not be at the same level of religious maturity as your partner, but each can be an encouragement to the other.

A couple may share their faith in God and have a similar commitment to Jesus Christ and yet have come from differing worship traditions. It is important that these differing traditions be shared and understood. You must be willing to communicate constantly and to compromise on nonessential matters. Try to find a common ground. Worship is a celebration of God. It is a good thing to celebrate together.

Mixed Marriage

People who marry outside their worship tradition may have to work extra hard to make a success of their relationship. The parents are usually their first serious problem. Parents know that marriage can be difficult in the best of circumstances and would prefer to see their child start out without this additional obstacle. In some extreme situations, a parent may refuse to have any part in the wedding. This puts a terrible strain on the relationship from the beginning.

The second serious problem is likely to crop up when the children arrive. When they come along, each parent begins to take more seriously his/her background of beliefs and values. It takes a very mature, loving couple to work out these differences.

The important thing is that the differences be faced realistically by both before marriage and that the couple comes to a solution to the problems before they enter marriage. Religious faith should enhance a marriage, not pull it apart.

Spiritual Pluses

A survey by a popular secular women's magazine found that religious women had better marriages, more sexual fulfillment, and better feelings about themselves than other women. The spiritual quality of life is a gift of God that we develop to our own benefit as well as that of others. The spiritual dimension has more to do with good health, marital fulfillment, and relationships than we can ever imagine. Truly spiritual people are not sad, pessimistic, boring people. They are joyous, exciting, adventurous, and courageous, with an ability to plow through troubled times without going to pieces. Spiritual maturity is worth the effort.

For You to Do

1. Tell each other your views on your faith. Describe some of your family's worship traditions.
2. If your fiancé(e) is of another faith, talk about how you will deal with this. Can you respect his/her religion? What about children? Parents?
3. How active are you in your church? Will your fiancé(e) be comfortable with this?
4. What makes life worth living to you? Share this with your partner.

20

Talk to Me About: Family Traditions

Family traditions become very important when you are contemplating marriage. All of the observances that can seem oppressive to rebelling adolescents seem special and significant when you are about to enter a permanent adult relationship. You are part of your parents' history. Their history was probably a combination of their own parents' history, and so it goes. Family histories, the way we celebrate, the way we mourn, the way we view mealtimes, are all important pieces of the puzzles of our individual lives. You will be combining your pieces of the puzzle to make a new picture, a new history of your own. You must take time to talk to each other about the parts of your life that are most important to you. You and your fiancé(e) will write most of the text for this chapter by writing your answers to questions about family patterns and traditions.

It is certainly true that couples who are interracial face more than the usual differences in many areas, as do Catholics married to Protestants, and Jews married to non-Jews. If you are in one of these categories, take the extra time to patiently listen to each other's family history and traditions. Decide how to deal with the differences while respecting the backgrounds of both families. To exist without a framework of history makes life in the present more difficult.

Holiday Hysteria

Holidays can be traumatic in your first year of marriage. Thanksgiving and Christmas are very tradition-laden for many families. Our older son is married to a wonderful German girl and they live in West Germany. His first Thanksgiving there was shocking for him. Since it is an American holiday, the Germans (to his thinking) totally ignored this wonderful opportunity for a turkey dinner. At Christmastime, to his great dismay, the family Christmas dinner was not held on December 25, nor did it feature the turkey and other fixings so special to the Self family. It is interesting what becomes important to you when it is suddenly not available.

Wendy's family Christmas tree was always a beauty. It filled up the two-story entrance hall and was always decorated in a theme. They had moved from the large multicolored lights to the clear, tiny, twinkling ones nestled among same-colored ribbons and satin balls. Brian's family tree was sometimes so lopsided that it had to be braced in order to keep its balance. There were handmade ornaments from each child's pre-school days. The lights were ancient red, green, and yellow ones that cast strange shadows on the tinsel and angel hair.

As their first Christmas approached, Wendy began to talk about their first Christmas tree and begged Brian to go with her to pick out the tree, the ornaments, and the lights. He did, and they wound up having the biggest argument of their married life. He simply couldn't see what was wrong with the big lights. What was a tree without them? She wouldn't be caught dead with tacky, old-fashioned lights. It was not an easy compromise.

As if the tree-and-lights argument wasn't bad enough, the worst was yet to come. Of course they would spend Christmas Eve with Wendy's parents and be there to open gifts Christmas morning. But Brian's family always made a big deal of Christmas morning, too; he really wanted to be with them. After all, they had spent Thanksgiving with Wendy's parents. What were they to do?

It's not easy to grow up and be away from home on special holidays. Family traditions always seem more special when we fear being separated from them. The time will come when

Wendy and Brian will decide to begin their own traditions in their own home. What would help now would be for Wendy's mother to stop whining and manipulating Wendy in the fall: "Of course you and Brian will be here for Christmas day"; or, "We're planning to get that dining room table for you, so of course you'll be here." And Brian's parents shouldn't heap guilt on him: "Well, it would be nice if we could all be together one more time." Holidays too often turn out to be stressful times. Try to be reasonable and fair!

Your Anniversary

How will you celebrate your anniversary? Some couples are very "ho hum" about the day while others celebrate in very creative ways. Remember that special occasions require planning. You will want to consider the meaning the anniversary has for you and communicate that to your spouse. Your first anniversary celebration will set a precedent for future anniversaries, so if you celebrate in a big way, the occasion will always be an important one. However, if you don't make it special in any particular way, then it will probably be assumed that you don't care to celebrate any differently in the future. You will need to communicate about this if you want to change the pattern.

A celebration does not necessarily have to be expensive in order to be meaningful to both of you. One couple I know always plays the videotape of their wedding ceremony. They say that it is a good reminder of the special feelings they had at their wedding and helps them focus on making this anniversary significant.

Mealtimes

Many families have fond memories built around the family dinner table. It is strange that in recent years everyone is so busy that it seems impossible for the family to eat a meal together. Home becomes a filling station, and no one bothers to stop long enough to sit down together. People resort to leaving notes on the refrigerator as their major means of communication. Unless one is traveling, you should plan to have at least one meal a day together. Communion as well as communication takes place at the table.

Don't let special occasions go by without some sort of celebration. These holidays, anniversaries, and birthdays are pleasant punctuation points in a sometimes drab life. Be creative in making these occasions significant events.

For You to Do

1. Tell each other about your holidays as you grew up. What stands out in your memory?
2. Tell each other about your favorite Christmas (or other holiday).
3. Do you have sad memories connected with holidays? Tell about them.
4. Can you decide where to spend Thanksgiving and Christmas this year?
5. Talk about the holiday budget. This includes traveling expenses as well as money for decorations and gifts.
6. Birthdays are an important event in many families. Tell each other how your family celebrated birthdays and if you feel that it is important to continue this tradition in your own family.
7. Agree to talk about your anniversary well in advance of the occasion so that you will both feel satisfied about the way you choose to celebrate.

21

Talk to Me About: Having Children

Until recently, nobody questioned the connection between "love and marriage, kids and carriage." It was a package deal. People assumed that not too long after a couple married, they would begin having children. If they did not, it was assumed that they were not able to conceive, not that they *chose* not to have a child.

Beginning in the 1960s, people have been challenging the assumption that "all married couples should have children." There has been an emphasis on zero population growth and this, as well as other considerations, has led couples to reconsider children as an automatic part of marriage. Many women became very career-oriented and postponed motherhood to concentrate on that facet of life. The longer they wait, the more likely they are to forgo it altogether.

Certainly, the majority of couples understand that the question of parenthood should be thoroughly discussed with some agreement reached before marriage. If one or the other is determined not to have children and the other feels strongly that he/she must have them, we suggest that you seek counseling, realizing that one may totally change his/her attitude about this matter after a while.

Why Have Children?

What does having children mean to a marriage? Of course, it will mean different things to each couple. However, there are some universal things, contradictory things, that a child will mean. It means that you will experience a different kind of love than you ever felt before, a love that lets you know that without a doubt, you could give up your life for this human being. You will experience the extremes of love, rage, fear, and frustration that only parents can know. It means you will know restrictions that bind you so tightly you feel that you can never escape. At the same time you will experience life's deepest joys. Children can bring a couple closer than they ever thought possible, and they also can split a couple further apart than one could ever imagine. Never succumb to the idea that if your marriage is not going well, having a baby will bring you closer. First of all, it will not help a sick marriage, and second, it is an unfair burden to place on any unsuspecting baby! Children change marriages and marriages affect children for years to come.

Planning Parenthood

Several couples we interviewed had babies early in the marriage. None of them had regrets about the children, but all wished they had had more time alone before their first child, or had been more aware of what a child would mean in their marriage. Changing attitudes about having a child out of choice rather than social obligation has probably added more meaning to having a child, possibly allowing parents to be more whole-heartedly dedicated to the child. A couple beginning with a conscious plan for the structure of their lives will not be able to eliminate all of the problems of child rearing, but some of the frustrations, anger, and feelings of entrapment will be eased. Just remember that there is never "the perfect time." Sometimes nature's timetable has to take precedence over perfect timing.

The decision to become parents is different from all other decisions. It is a decision that involves risk (how will you feel about being a parent; what will your child look like or act like at any given age, etc.) and permanence. It will be the most absorbing, life-defining, creative decision that you will ever make. What surprises are ahead!

It is not unusual today for one spouse (or both) to have great reservations about parenting. There are many reasons for this and we will touch on just a few, so that you can identify your feelings and communicate your misgivings. After you are married, these feelings may vanish; others may appear to fill the gap.

Parenting Readiness

First, you will need to think about health considerations. Take time to explore the possible problems in having a healthy baby. Is there anything in either of your family backgrounds that may be a risk factor? Also, *before* pregnancy occurs, the woman should be willing to abstain from *any* alcohol, drugs, or cigarettes. These things can increase dramatically the risk of deformed, brain-damaged, undernourished babies. The damage can be fatal in the first few weeks of pregnancy.

Next, can you afford a baby? Probably not! You'll never be able to "save up" for a baby but you will want to make some financial arrangements so that the stress level will be lower. Don't forget to consider whether or not you plan for the mother to continue to work: full time? part time? How soon after the birth of the baby will the mother return to work? These and other related questions (child care) require advance planning.

Some women can't believe that they may experience an overwhelming desire to stay at home with the baby. They are unprepared for the overpowering love they feel for this baby. So many young women have said, "Nobody told me I would love this baby so much." Well, someone may have at least implied it, but it is hard for anyone to understand until they have experienced it.

If you are uncertain about whether you want to have children, you should not feel pressured by friends or family. After all, you are the ones who will be responsible emotionally, physically, financially, and every other way for a baby. It is not like a part-time job or an extracurricular activity. A baby will absorb every moment, waking and sleeping, of your life.

Spend some time around young children, help out in your church nursery, give a friend a night out while you baby-sit.

Give yourselves a chance to find out how wonderful children can be.

Parenting Rewards

Someone has said that babies are a gift from God, sprinkled with stardust. They will make you stand in awe, view life from a different viewpoint, make you more human and understanding of others, and develop patience and skills heretofore unknown! It is an exciting, rewarding, permanent adventure, should you choose to experience it.

Once you have a child, everything in life changes. Rearing a child means learning new things, adding richness and excitement to marriage and to all of life. There will never be a dull moment. There will be hours of intense, single-minded absorption which are also times of intense attachment between partners. A child brings a certain intimacy and closeness between parents when they see glimpses of each other as a child. Parents have an opportunity to retrace their own childhood and that of their spouse through the children. This in itself is a bonding, just as caring for children together forms a unique tie that can bring the partners great pleasure and satisfaction. There are levels of joy and pain that one will never know without being a parent.

Realism in Parenting

As we mentioned in the previous paragraph, once you have a child, everything is different. That includes grocery shopping. One of my most vivid memories took place in the grocery store. Our sons were barely eighteen months apart in age and at times it was like having twins. Bryan was about ten months old; Lee was a little over two and deep into the "Terrible Two's." I had them both in the grocery cart and battled Lee on every aisle. He wanted everything, and explanations did not set well with him that day. I was just about finished (in more than one way!) and rounding the last aisle to the checkout counter when he made his last-ditch stand. I feel sure that Lee could out-tantrum any child in the world. In desperation, I turned to the first safe-looking, grandmotherly type woman I saw, thrust Bryan into her arms, and said, "Please hold him until I get back." I wrestled Lee to the car, locked the door, ran back to get Bryan from the startled lady, deserted my cart, and drove home entirely engulfed by screaming children, vowing that no matter how bare the cupboard, I would never again take both of them to the store at the same time. Bill and I agreed that I would pay a baby-sitter to stay with them so that I could shop for groceries in peace.

Yet I wouldn't miss the deep joy of hearing our sons' bedtime prayers, roaming the beach in search of the perfect shell, or hearing the voice of Bryan on the phone from the mountains saying, "Mom, you ought to see this sunset!" The satisfactions of parenthood far outweigh the negatives.

One young couple we know just had twins after six years of marriage. We volunteered to baby-sit so that they could get out. Where do you think they went? To the hardware store, the grocery store, and finally, to dine on fast food! Little things mean a lot under those circumstances!

Evelyn and Jack are now in their forties. Both have exciting careers and are active in many civic and church programs. When they met in the sixties, Evelyn did not intend to ever marry. She knew she wanted to be free to develop a career and felt there would be no room for family life. Jack persuaded her to marry him with the understanding that they would each be free to pursue their individual careers. This included a decision never to have children.

During one of our panel discussions on dual-career marriages, someone asked them if they had ever regretted that decision. Evelyn's answer was a resounding "No!" Jack was slower to answer and said that the year he turned forty was very painful to him; he had to do some soul-searching on this matter. He has accepted their decision and enjoys their nieces and nephews in a special relationship, but he has experienced moments of uneasiness that Evelyn seems not to have had.

Perhaps if you agree not to have children, you should look at your decision again before it is too late to change. It could be that one partner has developed doubts and is afraid to upset the other, but if you agree to open the discussion again at an appointed time (perhaps at a specific birthday), you'll have the opportunity to make sure that you are both still comfortable with your original decision. The passing of time and the deepening of your relationship may change your attitude.

If, for some reason, you are unable to have children, please try not to become obsessive about it. Many people have wonderful adopted children. The chances you take with adoption are probably no greater than having your own. Remember why you got married to begin with. Did you not plan to marry because you wanted desperately to be together? You have each other, and if you never have children, you will be able to creatively enhance your life in other ways.

For You to Do
Talk to each other about these things:

1. Do you want to have children?
2. When do you want to plan to start your family? Is age a reason for planning to have children soon after marriage?
3. Is your financial security dependent on two incomes?
4. Can you agree on how you will work out child care and careers?
5. Can you respond appropriately if your chosen method of birth control fails and an unplanned pregnancy occurs?
6. As the female, will you be willing to abstain from alcohol, drugs, and cigarettes during pregnancy to give your baby a fair chance?
7. Will either of you be devastated if it is not possible for you to bear children?

22

Blended Families: How Will You Relate to Spouse/Children of a Previous Marriage?

There are more and more people remarrying these days. Some of these second marriages follow the death of a spouse, but usually they follow a divorce. For a successful second marriage, the first requirement is for the divorced person to be sure that he/she has gone through the healing process. Too often one remarries before enough time has elapsed to allow the pain to be healed. Many times it is easier for a widow or widower to recuperate than it is for a divorced person. This is because death brings a complete and total break. There is no hope on earth for being reunited, no chance of seeing the departed spouse or having to deal with him/her because of children. There is anger involved in both death and divorce, but healing comes about in different ways. There are many good books available to help individuals in both of these situations. It is helpful to join a support group to augment personal counseling.

Is It Right to Remarry?

Many Christians who are divorced feel unclean and unworthy. Sometimes people who are contemplating marriage to a divorced person want assurance that it is all right. Some children of divorced parents have had to endure their church friends' ridicule when a parent remarries. "Living in sin" is an expression that could describe any person who harbors any sin for which he has not asked God's forgiveness. Imperfect people enter into marriage covenants and sometimes fail. There are many reasons for such failure. This is a very obvious missing of the mark and falling short of the glory of God, but it is not unpardonable.

If you are past the grieving stage and are sure that you are emotionally ready for a new marriage, there are a number of things to seriously consider. We have already discussed the financial aspect of a remarriage. This will be crucial to the success of your relationship.

Start Fresh!

Do each other the favor of making every effort to begin anew in this relationship. It may be difficult to trust your spouse because of your previous experience, but don't make your new relationship suffer because of past difficulties.

Be sure that your self-esteem is healthy. This will ensure that you are able to love yourself and relate to your new spouse in a mature way.

If there are children still living at home, there are other possible complications. Here are some examples:

- Before you marry, you should discuss how involved each will be in child care. You need to know how often and to what extent you will be expected to entertain stepchildren. You should make it known before marriage if you want to be very much involved in their care. It is better not to have too many surprises concerning children. Remember that marriage was intended for only two people! The more people involved, the greater the risks for trouble.

  One man who married a woman with three small children immediately took it upon himself to be the primary disciplinarian. Naturally, the children were upset. They began having serious sleeping problems and started acting out in school. Their real father finally discovered that the new husband was punishing his children by hitting them with a belt. These children were normally sweet and gentle; they certainly didn't deserve that kind of treatment. Finally, the mother divorced the second husband to remove her children from this frightening situation. The children are now in high school but she has never remarried. The pain of that period required a lot of therapy and assurances of her love for the children. Fortunately, they have adjusted well since that time.

- Allow children time to get used to the idea of a new person in their orbit. They need time to get to know this intended family member.

Tom and Jane married about ten years ago. Jane had never been married and had a wonderful career (she owned her own travel agency). Tom's first wife had died of cancer and left him with a grown son and ten-year-old daughter. When Tom and Jane met, they knew that they were meant for each other. Tom wanted to get married right away, but Jane insisted on waiting a while so that she could get to know the little girl, Lori. It was a long-distance romance, but Jane really spent more time with Lori, both alone and in the presence of Tom, than she did with him. Lori was finally the one who said, "Please marry my daddy so that I can call you Mom."

- Encourage your children to talk about their feelings. Try to respond to their fears or anger with understanding. They may feel that they are betraying the other parent if they like this new "replacement." Children need to feel understood and be understood.
- Discuss your ideas about child rearing with your fiancé(e). Be sure you let your spouse know how you would like to be supported in your parental role.
- Children should have private time with their natural parent. There will be less resentment on their part if they can be assured that they are not losing him or her.

We have observed the way a number of blended families have meshed the children from previous marriages. The most successful arrangements have been for his children to visit on the weekends that her children are with their own father. "Visit" is the appropriate word to use because the every-other-weekend children are really just visitors. They are treated different from the ones who live there full time.

The blending of the two is very difficult and rarely satisfactory. It is only natural that jealousy and frustration and probably quite a bit of anger will be present when blending is desired by the parents. Be fair and put yourself in their position. How would you react? We expect a lot out of our children that we would never expect of ourselves. It takes great skill, a positive attitude, a lot of love and even more patience to make it work. Enter the situation knowing that it will not be perfect . . . neither are families that have not been disrupted.

- After your marriage, you will need to present a united front to your children and others. Do not allow guilt to keep you from building a bond with your new spouse. Your child will feel more comfortable if he knows that the adults in his life are together. Your spouse should come first.

The most successful remarriage that we know about is a beautiful story. Jean had never been married and is almost fourteen years younger than Ed. His first marriage, to an alcoholic wife, had been tumultuous. When he continuously came home to find her in a stupor and his very young children uncared for, he finally got a divorce with custody of the children. When Ed and Jean married, the children were about six and ten years old. The six-year-old was looking for a mother and Jean was all she could want. The older child, a boy, had a harder time but nothing extremely serious. Ed and Jean very quickly had two more children and through the years, the four children of the family have been very close and loving. Jean has enough mother love for all of them and seems to show no difference in her feelings for her own two and her stepchildren. She mothers them all and takes care of every need. They are all grown and married now and Jean is the happiest grandmother we know.

Children's Adjustment

Children who are older, away at college, or married present another set of problems. They should be happy for you and, given time to adjust, they will be, unless it has been a traumatic divorce situation. Only time and patience can bring healing in that case. Grown children also need reassurances concerning their inheritance and your love for them. These things need to be discussed before you remarry.

Too often people who remarry expect everything to be perfect. They desire for all sides to get along beautifully and for all to live happily ever after. Yet this rarely happens even in first-marriage families. Personalities clash, disagreements occur, rules are debated, harsh words spoken. But strong families can handle all of this and more. Hang in there with a united front!

For You to Do

Answer these questions and discuss them with each other:

1. How long have you been widowed? Divorced?
2. Have you been in a support group? For how long?
3. Have you had counseling? When and for how long?
4. Have you emotionally cut the cord with your former spouse?
5. Have you told your fiancé(e) about financial arrangements concerning your children and former spouse?
6. Do you feel that you can deal with these arrangements and the reminders of your fiancé(e)'s past life?
7. If there are children involved: Do you like them? Do you want to make the effort to become involved and partially responsible for them? Can you deal with your spouse having this bond with his/her former spouse? Are you able to be open-minded about your spouse's feelings toward your children?
8. How are you going to make this marriage different from your previous marriage (in the case of divorce)? Have you determined the problem areas and made an effort to make appropriate changes?
9. Are you aware that even though logic would tell you that remarriages should work, the divorce rate is higher than for first marriages?
10. Do you plan to have children? How will this impact the current emotional and financial situation?
11. Why do you want to marry your fiancé(e)?

23

Talk to Me About: Alcohol and Substance Use/Abuse

Many of you will look at the title of this chapter and say, "We don't even need to read this because we do not have an alcohol or drug problem." I hope that is the truth, but it will still be a good idea for you to talk to each other about your attitudes concerning this topic. You will want to know about the other's family background in regard to alcohol and drugs because it could affect your future life.

Young adults today have come through the years when high school and college peers were deep into marijuana, cocaine, alcohol, and other drugs. You either experimented, became a weekend abuser, or had friends who did so, perhaps even becoming addicted. If you have alcohol or drug abuse in your background, your spouse-to-be needs to know.

This is the day of the young executive dealing in cocaine. The results are scary. There are at least 4 to 5 million Americans who regularly (at least monthly) use cocaine.

The results psychologically, mentally, and physically are so debilitating that anyone who is thinking about marrying a cocaine user should run away fast. You will learn that you cannot deal logically with a person who uses cocaine (or any other addictive drug), and your love will not bring about the needed changes. The best thing you can do for an abuser is to insist on his/her getting professional help. You are too close to be able to handle the situation. Do not become an "enabler," one who unwittingly but lovingly protects and cares for the abuser. There are agencies such as Alcoholics Anonymous to help you understand the problem and how you can help. If you suspect that your fiancé(e) has a problem, educate yourself on the substance and decide how involved you want to be.

Alcohol Abuse

Alcohol is a tricky substance. Some people seem to have no problem with it. Alcohol's effect on a person will be determined by many things. The younger a person is when he starts to drink, the more likely he is to develop problems later in life. Children of alcoholics are at least four times as likely to have drinking problems as others. The nervous system of each individual responds differently to ethanol, the active ingredient in alcoholic drinks. There are 18 million Americans with a drinking problem. That problem becomes a problem for all the people around him/her: spouse, parents, children, other family, friends, business associates, and unsuspecting persons on the highway.

Ethanol has a harmful effect on nearly every organ in the body. Chronic heavy drinking increases the risk of heart disease and high blood pressure. Alcohol eats away at the stomach and intestines. Alcoholic males may experience shrunken testes, reduced testosterone levels, and possibly impotence, while sustained drinking may disrupt women's menstrual cycles and render them infertile. Expectant mothers who drink can produce babies with serious birth defects and mental retardation. The efficiency of the immune system is also diminished. Studies are being done to determine whether heavy drinking might cause AIDS to surface more quickly in infected carriers. The worst toll is on the liver, where most of the ethanol in the bloodstream is broken down. There is a slow poisoning of the liver and this degeneration of the liver (cirrhosis) affects at least ten percent of all alcoholics. It is especially hard on women, even if they consume less alcohol.

Knowing the terrible things that alcohol does to human beings, it is amazing that intelligent people deny that they are headed for trouble and wind up using alcohol (as well as other drugs) as a crutch when life gets difficult. No one is immune to the possibility that he/she could become an alcoholic.

Children of Alcoholics

Adult children of alcoholics have special problems to overcome. Not only are they more prone to the disease themselves, but they are still dealing with a lot of childhood hurts that may be covered by a kind of childish loyalty to the parent. They may suffer from feelings of guilt, though they were certainly not to blame for the problem of their parents. The child of alcoholic parents is an abused child emotionally, if not physically, and needs to participate in group therapy.

Who is an alcoholic? That is a tricky question with no absolute answer. The extreme cases are clearcut. There are physical, psychological, and behavioral problems that are pretty obvious. However, when a person's activities, attitude, and health take their toll on those around him/her, it can be assumed that there is an alcohol problem that requires professional help to control. An alcoholic or substance-addicted person may think that it is no one else's business but his own. But there is an ever-widening circle of people who are affected and influenced by the person with the problem.

Social Drinking

The average person is often faced with the situation of "social drinking." At one time, a person who refused an alcoholic drink at a party was ridiculed. People who were trying to get ahead in the business world were sometimes at a disadvantage if they did not serve alcohol. With the growing public outcry against drunken drivers and the placing of some of the responsibility on their hosts, it has become socially acceptable to serve nonalcoholic drinks. The number of celebrities who have publicly admitted that they have changed their drinking habits has made it easier for others to abstain or at least show restraint in this area.

We still see teenagers and others using beer as a soft drink, thinking that the alcohol will not affect them. But alcohol is alcohol; its effect on the brain is the same whether it is found in beer or vodka.

We have all heard someone say, "I am not as shy after I have a cocktail. It is easier for me to talk to people." It would be a lot safer for you to work on developing your personality and learning what makes a person likable, how to be a good listener, and how to care about people. Those are qualities that will earn you an invitation to parties. What's more, you'll know what is going on and get home safely.

I just talked to a friend whose teenage daughter was in the car of a friend who was driving under the influence. The driver hit another car and was killed instantly, while the driver of the second car will be paralyzed for life. A couple of beers turned deadly.

As a couple who will be entertaining, you should learn to serve some delicious and interesting nonalcoholic drinks. Don't be afraid to be the pacesetter in this serious matter. The life you save may be your own!

The problem of alcohol and drug abuse is growing in our nation. We can never assume that we or our loved ones will escape this type of pain. But if you know the facts and act sensibly and responsibly, you will be way ahead.

For You to Do

1. Are you the child of an alcoholic parent? Have you been in therapy to help you deal with this? Have you resolved your feelings of guilt and anger?
2. Tell each other about the attitudes concerning alcohol and/or drugs in your home.
3. Write down how much alcohol (including beer) you consume and your use of drugs (marijuana, cocaine, heroin, prescription drugs, etc.). Show this to your fiancé(e). Do either of you feel that this is an excessive amount?
4. If you consume alcohol or use drugs, ask your fiancé(e) if he/she is ever alarmed or afraid of you when you are "under the influence."
5. Are you willing to educate yourself on this matter and think seriously about what you may be doing to your body? Do you love your future spouse enough to make changes?

24

Good Advice

Here we are at the end of the book. You may be wondering if you really want to get married after all! We hope that if you do have a question, you'll take a little longer before setting the wedding date.

Our church sponsors a class especially for couples who are "just married" through their second anniversary. I asked this group to write down their answer to: "I wish I had known . . ." or "My advice . . ." for those who are about to be married. Their responses are listed below. (There were a few more responses from the wives than the husbands.)

WIVES:
"I wish someone had explained that it is not wrong to say 'no' to the proposal if you have doubts, even if it hurts his feelings now."

"My advice is: If it doesn't feel right and deep down inside you know it's not right, DON'T do it. It's worth it to back out even if invitations have gone out and the gifts are coming in."

"I wish I had known that if you do something once, you'll be expected to do it for the rest of your life (i.e., cut the grass, pay the bills, etc.)."

"I wish I had known what his family valued (i.e., mealtime was important, a clean house, church). My advice is: Do not live near the in-laws."

"My advice is: Don't feel like you have to change yourself to fit in with his family."

"I wish I had known that he likes to sleep with the television on."

"I wish I had known that buying a home is more stressful than getting married."

"I wish someone had told me: (1) Don't have any expectations. (2) Don't try to change each other. (3) Work together. (4) Don't rush things. (5) Never go to bed mad."

"I wish I had known that the responsibility was more than I ever imagined and that you are not #1 in your life anymore. . . . The #1 position is shared by your mate."

"I wish I had known more about my spouse's ideas about money. We have very different ideas on making major purchases. We know how to compromise, but sometimes it gets a little heated. My advice is to learn to fight in the proper way. Remember during a 'discussion' that your marriage is first! If you are fighting in order to come to a conclusion to better your marriage, you're on the right track."

"I wish someone had told me that marriage does not come naturally. It takes constant communication and compromise and can never be taken for granted."

"I wish I had known how much patience it takes getting to know each other's habits and living styles."

"I wish I had known we had such different thought processes. I wish I had known that his idea of taking out the trash and mine were so different. My advice: Don't take things too seriously. Laugh through it!"

"I wish I had known what an impact family influences can make on a person. The way one partner does or doesn't do something (for the most part) is determined by how his family handled the same or similar situations."

"My advice: Learn to be flexible! Compromise."

"My advice about marriage would be to eliminate selfish pride and always be willing to compromise. This can eliminate a lot of unnecessary arguments."

"I wish I had realized that if a person thinks poorly of himself before marriage, it will remain the same. I thought that marrying me would give him the needed incentive to make something of himself. It hasn't."

"My advice is: Never take your spouse for granted. Never try to change each other . . . you'd better like him the way he is *before* marriage."

"I wish I had known how truly wonderful it was to share your life with someone and that it is o.k. to trust him with even your most private thoughts. Trusting someone in this way is a great feeling and makes the bond between you stronger. My advice: Always be honest no matter what the situation. Continue to maintain your own identity throughout your marriage."

HUSBANDS:

"I wish I had known that some of the things that are important to one spouse do not necessarily make the top five list of things important to another . . . clean house, clean kitchen. And why didn't someone tell me that in-laws can make holidays tough?"

"I wish I had known that my single friends would feel as if they were 'losing' me to marriage. Activities with single friends may be less frequent. The singles' schedules are much more flexible."

"I wish I had known how much hard work is involved. My advice: (1) Keep Christ at center of home. (2) Communicate! (3) Tell spouse you love her . . . often. (4) Be patient!"

"I wish I had known the work involved in keeping a house and yard clean."

"My advice: *Understand* each other's feelings on money, family, religion, and realize they probably won't change."

"I wish I had known about those unpaid credit cards!"

"My advice is to make the church and the friends you make there a central part of your lives. This will help tremendously in resisting the negative external influences we face each day."

"My advice is to let one person handle the financial business such as checking accounts and paying bills. Eat crow if you have to!"

"My advice is to have fun and enjoy every moment together. Be willing to compromise and see things the way your spouse may see them."

"I wish I had known how to express emotions and feelings better. Why didn't someone tell me how important communication is to a marriage and how expressing expectations is the basis for good communication? My advice would be to have a three- to five-month counseling period with a professional counselor. Marriage is wonderful!"

"I wish I had known how hard marriage would be. It is a lot of work to be respectful of each other all the time. But it is worth every bit of effort it takes!"

"I wish I had known that marriage was so wonderful and rewarding."

As you can see, these observations run from the ridiculous to the sublime. However, if it was important enough for the person to write down, it is worth reading. I was saddened that several of the females seemed so desperately sorry that they got married. You, as an engaged couple using this book, have the advantage of looking at all the areas that are potential trouble-makers. You won't have all the answers, but at least you won't be surprised when you encounter difficulty. One more note of warning before we go on to happier thoughts: There are worse things than being single . . . one is being married to the wrong person.

The Diamond Ring

There are a lot of popular songs written about love. One of the older ones describes love as a "many splendored thing." It really is. It is like the many facets of a diamond, each catching and reflecting the light, sparkling and splendid to behold. Love is the magnificent diamond while marriage is the setting that holds it. The setting has to be maintained and polished and made of precious metal. Love and marriage do go together. One without the other is not much good. We hope that you will view your relationship as an expensive diamond in a setting of precious metal. As a diamond ring is round, so it is with your love . . . it has no end. There are as many facets in your diamond as there are variations of your personalities. Keep it in good condition, cleaned and polished, shining bright for all the world to view.

Remember also that not only do you love each other, but you should *like* each other. "Like" is as important as love in a marriage. You'll treasure the time you have together because you are not only lovers but best friends, too. You'll be giving advice to engaged couples in a year or so and you will agree with the young man who said, "Marriage is wonderful!"

To each of you who work your way through this book and proceed down the aisle, we wish for you the surprises and delights, the pleasures and deep joys of a loving relationship. May God richly bless you as you enter the "enchanting bonds of matrimony."

Suggestions for Group Activities

It is important that each person in your group feel comfortable. For the first few minutes, have them chat among themselves while you observe the group interaction. As they take their places (chairs should be in a circle or semicircle), have each one introduce him or herself and tell how they met and when they plan to marry.

Chapter 1

As the leader, you should take a few minutes to explain the purpose of the seminar and encourage their presence and participation.

In order to get them to participate rather than just listen to you lecture, ask this or a similar question: "What is your definition of marriage?" Direct the discussion so that no one person dominates; perhaps asking other questions will lead to your goal. Conclude the session on time so that they will learn to be on time themselves. Make sure they know that you expect them to do the work at the end of each chapter.

Chapter 2

Start the session by asking, "Are family tensions beginning to escalate as the wedding date approaches? Whose wedding is it anyway . . . yours or your parents?" This will give the group an opportunity to realize that almost every family reacts the same way to important occasions. Talk about ways to ease the tensions and make it a happy occasion.

Chapter 3

Begin in small groups, with each person in the group giving a brief answer to this question: "When you were a child, what was one of the most loving things someone did for you?" As you return to the larger group, have one or two repeat their stories; perhaps you will share your story with the group. This will set the tone for the discussion of what real love is.

Chapter 4

At the beginning of the study of chapter 4, ask each person to tell the group something significant about themselves. You should be prepared to lead the way. For example, "I am a gourmet cook," or, "I am good at getting organized." Too often people attach their self-worth to someone else. Example: "I have a son who is a star football player."

Chapter 5

In this chapter you can suggest that people can change, and quite often SHOULD change. "I can never trust anybody because my father deserted me when I was a child." "I can't help being this way. My mother wouldn't let me have an ice-cream cone one day when I was seven years old." Sounds silly, doesn't it, but we blame our weird ways on the past. It is called scapegoating.

One way to create interest and to get participation from the group is to divide them into groups of not more than five people (not couples), with a mix of male and female in each. Have each person tell the group very briefly how they see their relationship with their family (are they dependent; are they a close-knit unit; do they think their spouse-to-be will fit in?). Direct the groups to make some positive suggestions as to how they can help the new relationship (new spouse and in-law family) develop smoothly. Report back to the group as a whole. As the leader you can make comments and suggestions.

Chapter 6

Ask each person to write down his/her reason for getting married. Provide paper and pencil so that the answers cannot be identified by differences in paper or ink. Assure them before they begin that no one will know the author of their statements. The only identifying mark should be an F or M to designate male or female. Collect the papers and distribute them male to male and female to female, being sure that no one gets his/her own. Then have each person read what is written on the paper. Your guidance will be needed to cover the material.

Chapter 7

Divide your class into two groups, with no couples in the same group. Keep the groups mixed, male and female. Have both groups brainstorm the same question, each bringing back to the large group the results of their discussion. Use their reports as the springboard for your comments. The question: "How do you know when you are ready to get married? What are some specifics that need to be considered?"

Chapter 8

It is important to discuss breaking an engagement at least briefly because couples need to know that it is better to break an engagement than to break up a marriage. We have had several couples decide to postpone marriage. One or two have later married, but most have gone separate ways. Couples need to understand that it is a sign of maturity if they handle it well.

Chapter 9

Divide your couples into several small groups, no more than five to a group, with no couples together. Give each group this question to discuss: "What does money mean to you?" Have one person in each group keep notes and report back to the larger group in about eight minutes. You may get some answers like: "Money can solve most problems." "Money means security." "The more money you have, the more successful you are." Direct the discussion toward the ideas in chapter 9. What their parents think of money plays a large part in what young people think of it.

Chapter 10

Have each couple turn toward each other so that they can talk without interruption. Explain that they are to list their needs, wants, and dreams. Needs are the things you must have, things you are going to do first. Wants are the second line of what is important to you. You'd like to have them but they can wait. Dreams are plans for the distant future. Dreams are important because they help us reach higher and keep us going on dreary days. When this is completed, have the group come together and relate how their needs, wants, and dreams can be achieved by facing the money situation realistically.

Chapter 11

Money is one of the major battles of a divorce. If you have any divorced or widowed people in your group, this is a very important topic. If there are only one or two such couples in your group, you may want to set up a special session with them to discuss this subject.

Role play is sometimes a good way to help people visualize situations that will demand their loyalty and understanding. You can make up a situation that will fit the needs of your constituents or adapt one of the following suggestions:

1. Mary and Dan have been married for almost two years and it has become increasingly difficult for Mary to be pleasant about the excessive financial demands that Dan's two teenage children are placing on him. She sees that most of her paycheck is going to pay for this obligation. She also sees that her desire to have a child is becoming less and less of a possibility as this situation continues. Have a Mary and a Dan role-play this situation to bring out all that is going on in the relationship. Offer some rational solutions.

2. Jack was well aware of the two children whom Sandra brought to their marriage. He is very fond of them and feels very "fatherly" toward them. However, he has difficulty with the fact that their real father is making little or no financial contribution for their needs. He can see that they will always be under a financial strain with very limited possibilities for vacations or better housing. He is feeling resentful. Through role play, devise some ways to communicate about this problem.

Chapter 12

Ask the group these questions, allowing time for response:

1. Do you think that it is important to have a family budget? Why or why not?
2. Who will write the checks to pay the bills in your family?
3. Do you plan to keep separate bank accounts? Why?

After appropriate discussion time, direct their thinking to the rest of the material in this chapter. Allow some time for the couples to discuss their concerns in this area.

Chapter 13

Communication style has been rated as one of the major causes of marital arguments. Couples need to learn to communicate in a way that is satisfactory to both. The time to begin this process is now. They should learn to say what they want to say so that each partner can understand.

Communicating well does not mean that there will be no discord. Every healthy marriage has some conflict, but the end result can be positive if the couple has learned how to fight fairly.

Ask your group: How often do you have fights or serious disagreements? How do you handle the conflicts? Are you open or do you clam up? Does one do all the talking? Be sure that couples complete the FOR YOU TO DO section.

Chapter 14

Using the small group system, give each one a different situation to brainstorm and offer suggestions for fighting fairly.

1. When I get angry, I become very caustic and enjoy attacking my opponent verbally. I know this hurts, but I can't seem to help it. My fiancé(e) withdraws, so we never get anything settled. I wish he/she would talk to me.
2. My family has always discussed everything explosively. When I am upset, I yell and vigorously state my case. Why does my fiancé(e) seem afraid of me?
3. I cannot handle fights. I hate conflict. It seems to be easier to go along rather than get involved in a fight. My fiancé(e) accuses me of being unfeeling. Actually, I guess I probably sulk and try to make him/her feel sorry for me. I like the attention.
4. When I get angry I just run away from the situation. Why bother to get all upset and try to explain my feelings? What difference will it make?
5. When my feelings are hurt, I can't help but cry. This upsets my fiancé(e) and he/she gets angry with me.

From these situations and others, get the group to set up some guidelines for fighting fairly.

Chapter 15

Dealing with intimacy is very important. Perhaps you as leader can best help by talking about marriage as a relationship of sharing and intimacy. There may be a tendency on the part of some partners to be "smothering" in their relationship. Just because a couple is married does not make them identical twins. When two people are deeply in love, they have a strong tendency to get as close together as possible. They must be careful not to make unreasonable demands on each other. It is important for each to have interests so that some spice can be added to the relationship. Lead the couples in discussing their ideas of intimacy. Use the suggestions in the book to help them think of ways to strengthen intimacy.

Chapter 16

If you know an obstetrician/gynecologist who could talk to your group, it would be helpful. If he/she makes the group feel comfortable, there will be a good response during the question and answer period. Be sure that the guest speaker talks about diseases (such as venereal diseases, AIDS, herpes). Case studies are always impressive. If you do not have anyone from the medical community, be prepared with articles and other information available from the public library and American Medical Association.

Chapter 17

Ask for volunteers to do some role play to begin the discussion. Have one couple (they do not necessarily have to be engaged to each other) give a short skit of what the "traditional" ("Father Knows Best") family was like in the 1950s. Have another couple role-play a modern version of partnership marriage. Remind the group that partnership marriage is not to be equated with dual-career marriages. There are some dual-career marriages where the wife chooses to stay at home in a beautiful picture of partnership.

Chapter 18

Divide your couples into groups of not more than six. Give each group a problem to solve and then report back to the large group. Here are some suggestions:

1. Joe's father died when he was four years old. He was an only child and his mother never remarried. She is very dependent on Joe for emotional support, has few friends of her own, and has indicated that she resents his approaching marriage. She has hinted rather broadly that she would like to have them live with her, and Joe is having difficulty making her understand that Beth is not interested in this arrangement. She has also let them know that they (Joe) must call her every day, and they should eat with her several times a week and certainly every Sunday. Beth is having second thoughts about this marriage. Should she be worried? How should Joe react to this situation? Offer suggestions for all three persons involved.
2. Jill's parents think that she is making a mistake in marrying Bob. He is not their "kind" and therefore not good enough for their daughter. They see that she is going through with the wedding but they use every opportunity to belittle him and point out his so-called weaknesses. Jill has always been close to her parents and feels torn between them and Bob. She feels badly about the way they treat him but makes no effort to stop it. How can this situation be helped?
3. Dan's parents are very wealthy and are generous with financial help. They are also generous with advice in all areas of his life. Now that he is engaged to Rhonda, they are including her in their generosity. Rhonda is from a working-class family and has always been very independent. She enjoys a promising career. She is uncomfortable with all the money and advice. She feels that there are too many strings attached. This situation is about to break up their engagement even though Dan and Rhonda love each other

very much. Can this situation be salvaged to the satisfaction of all concerned? How?

Chapter 19

By now you should know the makeup of your group and whether or not you have any "mixed marriages." Give them about eight minutes to tell each other privately about their religious experience or belief in God. Have them tell each other about the frequency of church attendance as a child and more recently.

Divide the group into sections not larger than five or six and have them discuss this question: "How important is religion in the success of a marriage? Give some reasons." Have them report back to the larger group so that they can hear the thoughts of many.

Very often it happens that a wife or husband will say after being married awhile, "I didn't know my husband (wife) was religious before I married him/her. We didn't discuss religion much. I didn't know it was such a big deal to him/her." This is a sad commentary on our lack of communication about this very serious matter. Young people often go through a rebellious, nonreligious phase and in a few years decide that they really do want to be a religious person. This type of change may or may not be welcomed by the spouse. It puts a different slant on a lot of things, including life-style.

People who are brought up in the same religious tradition, even when from different parts of the country, are better able to understand each other's religious language and expectations than those who are from wide-ranging traditions. Even if the person is going through a nonreligious stage right now, it is important to know his/her background.

A person who is sensitive and understanding about religion is more likely to be open to strengthening communication skills as well as developing a sense of intimacy. Religion is very personal and private. To be able to share that aspect of life is very precious.

You might begin the discussion by telling about a couple you know who have different religious backgrounds and how it is working for them Ask if anyone in the group knows someone in this category. Lead the discussion to draw out their own religious beliefs or traditions.

Chapter 20

Help each couple in your group talk to each other about their own ideas of celebrating holidays. Exhibit a joyful attitude about life in general. Use the following suggestions for your group.

Every family needs to celebrate often. Life gets routine and we get so bogged down with the details of living that we forget to have fun and celebrate. Don't wait until a legal holiday to celebrate . . . make your own holiday! At least once a week do something that is pure fun with each other and later as a family. We need special occasions to keep us from getting boring and from being bored.

Religious and national holidays give us the right to celebrate. Families have different ideas about what is appropriate for certain holidays. Be sure you discuss this now so that there will be fewer surprises later.

Decide on some special ways that you as a couple want to observe occasions such as birthdays, Thanksgiving, and Christmas. It is nice for each family unit to have their own special traditions.

This may also be a good time to talk about how often you expect or would like to go out to eat, to the movies, or to a play after you are married. If your expectations are different, you should face this now.

Chapter 21

Not long ago a friend told me that she was relieved to know that her son-in-law had changed his mind about not having children. When he and her daughter had been engaged, he was vehement about the matter. Her parents were concerned because they knew that their daughter would be miserable without having children. Many people change their minds about this after marriage, but it is important for them to discuss their present feelings while engaged. They need to know the honest desires of each other. Many times one or both will have serious doubts or fears about having children. Help your group to share their fears concerning this. Mention a few to get the discussion going (responsibility, lack of patience, loss of freedom, physical pain, child-care resources). Make sure that each couple makes use of the FOR YOU TO DO section.

Chapter 22

Dealing with spouses and children from a previous marriage can be one of the most difficult situations in life. It is very important to set up some ground rules for communicating *about* them and *with* them. If there are children from a former marriage, it will be hard for the "noncustodial" stepparent not to resent them. Urge those in your group to realize that this is common and suggest extra help with this type of situation.

Time and patience is the only solution in many cases. It is very important for the stepparent to know that he/she has the support and loyalty of the spouse. Too often the new spouse feels like an intruder with the former spouse and any children involved. Help those in your group to talk this through so that fears and problems can be realistically addressed now.

Chapter 23

Give your participants one or two of these life situations to think about and discuss. This will give you an opportunity to be sure that they understand the importance of alcohol and drug-related problems for family and career.

1. My family is from a very conservative, prohibitionist point of view where alcohol is concerned. I do not drink because I don't like the taste of beer or wine and I don't see why Stan insists on keeping beer in the refrigerator. It will embarrass me terribly if my parents ever know that he drinks and that his family serves wine and mixed drinks. They will think that I have lost my religion and good upbringing. This is a very touchy subject with us. How can we make this work?
2. John's family is very loving and caring but they seem to drink a lot, especially in times of stress. I know that John's uncle and grandfather died of cirrhosis of the liver and I am afraid that the tendency to alcoholism will affect John. I am not used to dealing with people who drink so much but I love John and don't want to lose him. Should I tell him how I feel?

Helps for Marriage Counselors
and Church School Leaders

Bible References

All Scripture quotations are from the New International Version of the Bible.

Chapter 1

Referring to God's relationship to the church and the relationship of husband and wife: Ephesians 5:21–31; Revelation 22:17; Matthew 9:15. This emphasizes the commitment in the marriage relationship. God uses the marriage relationship to define His relationship with the church, His Bride. He is committed to the church unconditionally. Apply this to marriage.

Chapter 2

Betrothal is an ancient term for being engaged. It has always been considered a very serious commitment. In Hosea 2:19, 20, God used the prophet Hosea's situation to say to Israel: "I will betroth you to me forever; I will betroth you to me in righteousness and justice, in love and compassion. I will betroth you in faithfulness. . . ."

Chapter 3

The Bible talks of four kinds of love: (1) God's love for us; (2) our love for God; (3) our love for our fellowman; (4) our love for ourselves. If any of these gets distorted, love is deficient in experience. For example, if one doesn't understand God's love, he cannot love himself. And if he cannot love himself, he cannot love his fellowman.

Agape love is the love that God has for each of us. "For God so loved the world that He gave His only begotten Son . . ." (John 3:16). This is sacrificial love that God Himself initiated and demonstrated. This agape love meets the requirements set forth in 1 Corinthians 13:4–8a.

Have each couple read 1 Corinthians 13:4–8a aloud to each other and discuss how this teaching should be applied to their relationship now and in the future.

Chapter 4

Genesis 1:27, 31; 5:1, 2. The word for "man" used in the creation account is the generic term for all mankind. The equality of person-hood is evident in the creation account. Each person, male or female, has infinite worth in God's eyes. God paid us His highest compliment by creating us in His own image. Use these Scriptures to reinforce the appropriateness of a healthy self-esteem. Also read Psalm 139 to emphasize the omnipresence and omniscience of God to His creation.

Chapter 5

Romans 14:7–12 and Galatians 6:7, 8 show that it is possible for people to make changes in their lives. We do not have to remain stuck with habits and attitudes that are not pleasing to God. Also, each person must realize that he/she will have to stand before God on his own. No one can do that for another person.

Chapter 6

Genesis 2:18; Galatians 6:2; 1 Thessalonians 5:11. Our relationship as husband and wife is to be helpful to each other as well as to be companions.

Chapters 9, 10, 11, 12

These four chapters on finances are very important. Money is often a spiritual problem and we need to understand that the Bible is not silent on this subject. We are taught in the Bible how to view money and possessions. Second Timothy states that we are to be in control of our money, rather than vice versa. Here are a few of the Bible verses that will help put the proper perspective on this issue:

Genesis 28:22; Ecclesiastes 5:10; Isaiah 55:2; Malachi 3:8–10; Matthew 6:24; Mark 8:36, 37; 2 Corinthians 9:7, 8; 1 Timothy 5:8; 1 Timothy 6:10, 17, 18; 1 John 3:17.

Help your group grapple with this important issue. Generous people are much happier and healthier than those who are stingy. Discuss the biblical teaching of tithing.

Chapter 13

Proverbs 10:12–14; Proverbs 12:17–19; Proverbs 15:1–4, 28; Proverbs 18:13; James 1:19, 20, 26; James 5:16; 1 Corinthians 13. Talking is the chief way we have of revealing ourselves to one another. Words can cause great pain or great joy. The Bible verses listed above are very clear in their meaning for us.

Chapter 14

Proverbs 15:18; Proverbs 16:32; Proverbs 17:14; Proverbs 19:11; Proverbs 25:28; Ecclesiastes 7:9; Ephesians 4:26, 29–32; James 1:19, 20. The Bible teaches that it is all right to be angry, to disagree, but to be careful that it is done properly without damaging the relationship. These Scriptures give sage advice.

Chapter 15

Matthew 19:4–6; Ephesians 5:28–33; 1 Corinthians 13:4–13; Song of Solomon 8:6, 7. People who come together in marriage have the hopes of an intimate relationship uppermost in their minds. This is the quality most longed for and the most difficult to attain. The words "sacrifice" and "commitment" are absolutely necessary for the type of intimacy desired. The ability to develop an intimate relationship with one's spouse is the gift of God, but if we desire it, we must work at it. Actually, we are falling short of what God has in mind for the marriage partnership when we fail to tenderly and lovingly work toward this goal. Someone has suggested that intimacy can be defined as the ability to give to one's partner without resentment, and in turn to receive from that partner without embarrassment. Partnership marriage offers the best opportunity for developing intimacy. A lesser relationship does not support the type of openness necessary for mutual nurturing.

Chapter 16

Use the Scriptures listed for chapters 3, 15, and 17. Also read 2 Samuel 11. This is the graphic story of what can happen to "good" people when overcome by desire. David was tempted, not by going out looking for trouble, but while doing what he normally did after dinner. Bathsheba was also absorbed in her evening ritual of bathing. David's indiscretion eventually led to murder and intrigue. The Bible does not try to hide the sins of God's people. We are to learn that no one is exempt from temptation and that if we yield, we have to be willing to pay the price.

Chapter 17

Galatians 3:28; Ephesians 5:25–33; 1 Corinthians 13. The New Testament world was male-dominated in every area. The family was patriarchal with the husband as the head. Translating the idea of headship into modern terms, the concept of *responsibility* is accepted by noted theologians. Authority is not domination but responsible headship for the family. When the husband accepts and acts on his responsibility in Christ, then he is worthy of trust and respect. Husbands were admonished to love their wives, a reactionary teaching in those days. And wives were instructed to respect their husbands. Since marriages were arranged and women were like chattel, this was a new concept. Dr. John Howell, author of *Equality and Submission in Marriage*, says that "it is impossible to love one's wife in accord with the biblical description of love without voluntarily surrendering an autocratic spirit of domination over her life. Instead, a man is to accept his wife as an *equal partner* in creating a marital relationship which honors that kind of love. The husband's voluntary yieldedness in love fulfills the command to be submissive or subordinate to one another in reverence for Christ."[1] Each marriage is different. Always be ready and open to grow and change. Cut your own pattern.

Chapter 18

Romans 12:18; Hebrews 12:14, 15; Ephesians 4:1, 2, 31, 32; Matthew 5:9. All of these verses deal with how we should relate to others. It would be especially helpful if we could treat family members with respect.

Chapter 19

Psalm 127:1; Daniel 6:10; Romans 8:28. A shared religious belief is important in a marriage. Too often this is the last thing that is discussed by couples contemplating marriage. One should never marry someone in order to "change" him or her. Faith is a personal and individual matter that cannot be forced. Religion and a church relationship become even more important when children arrive.

Chapter 20

Luke 2:1–20; Isaiah 9:6. Christmas is the Christian holiday that has the most religious and family significance. It is always difficult for children of a close-knit family to be away for the Christmas season. This causes trauma for many couples in their first few years of

1. John C. Howell, *Equality and Submission in Marriage* (Nashville: Broadman Press,1979). Italics were added for emphasis

marriage. Parents do not make this any easier. They often use manipulative ploys to make sure that all their children are under their roof, no matter how reluctant they may be. Perhaps it would be helpful if the newly married couple could sit down with parents and make plans that will be satisfactory. Parents should be urged to be cooperative and supportive in this.

Make sure that your Christmas traditions are truly Christian and that you are not forgetful of the spirit of love, goodwill, and generosity that should accompany the holiday.

Chapter 21

Ephesians 6:1–4; 2 Corinthians 12:14b; Proverbs 22:6; Matthew 18:1–6. Becoming a parent is something to consider seriously. Children are a gift from God, but many times people are not prepared to graciously receive this gift. When a child is awaited with great happiness and joy, the experience is one of overwhelming awe of God's love. Make this part of marriage an enriching religious experience. Take your new role as a parent seriously and be the best you can be.

Chapter 22

Ezekiel 18:22; Hebrews 4:16; Ephesians 4:29–32; Matthew 6:12, 14, 16; Romans 12:14; Colossians 3:13; 1 Peter 3:9; Matthew 7:1, 2. These Scriptures assure forgiveness and also instruct us not to be judgmental. It is important for the individual to forgive himself (herself) and to be kind and gentle in what may be unpleasant or difficult circumstances.

Chapter 23

Leviticus 10:9; Numbers 6:3; Proverbs 20:1; Proverbs 21:17; Proverbs 23:29–32; Isaiah 5:11; Isaiah 28:1; Hosea 4:11; Luke 1:15; Romans 14:21; Ephesians 5:18; 1 Timothy 5:23; Genesis 9:20; Genesis 14:18; John 2:1–9. All classes of Hebrews in Bible times used wine, with the exception of the Nazarites and the Rechabites. It was made by Noah, and used by Abraham. Jesus turned water into wine at a marriage feast, and Paul suggested its use as a medicinal remedy. Priests were required to abstain at certain times and prophets warned people against the excessive use of wine.

If you read with a discerning eye, the Old Testament shows that the problem of alcoholism is very old. Some people simply do not have the ability to drink in moderation. Reading Proverbs and other warnings makes it sound very uninviting, yet we have the same problem today. Christians should pay close attention to Romans 14:21. It is interesting to note that meat is included right along with wine in the admonition!

Be sure you understand that prescription drugs can also present a problem. It is important that people are on the alert for the first signs of addiction and are willing to take appropriate action.